ABERDEEN AT WORK

LORNA CORALL DEY & MICHAEL DEY

AMBERLEY

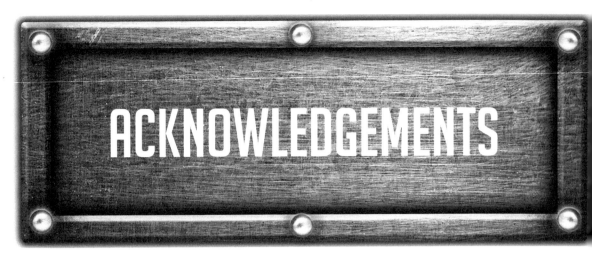

ACKNOWLEDGEMENTS

We gratefully acknowledge the assistance of the following individuals and organisations in preparation of this book: Sandy Wiseman, Seonaidh Baker and the Seven Incorporated Trades of Aberdeen; Jon Nicol and the Shore Porters Society; Ken Whittaker, Michael Robertson and Whittaker Engineering; Natalie Ghazi, Rahel Jones and Vatenfall; Heather Downer, Sarah Franklin, Alan Robertson and Jill Thomson.

First published 2020

Amberley Publishing
The Hill, Stroud
Gloucestershire, GL5 4EP

www.amberley-books.com

ISBN 978 1 4456 9668 3 (print)
ISBN 978 1 4456 9669 0 (ebook)

British Library Cataloguing in Publication Data. A catalogue record for this book is available from the British Library.

Origination by Amberley Publishing.
Printed in the UK.

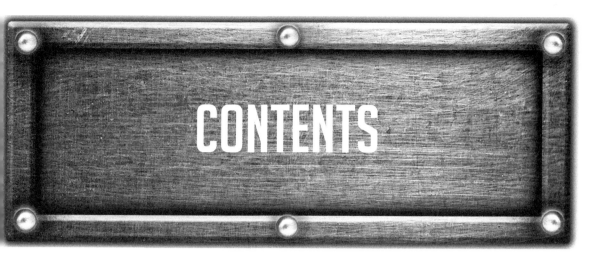

CONTENTS

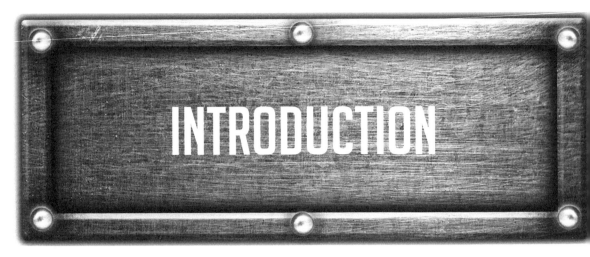

INTRODUCTION

Work is a small word, but one that resonates with deep historical meaning. At first glance it appears simple: work is work, what is difficult about that? Yet stop and think: the what, where, how and who are questions that require rounded answers. At the most basic of levels we can say work requires expenditure of energy, but within that catch-all lie differences such as between physical and cerebral work.

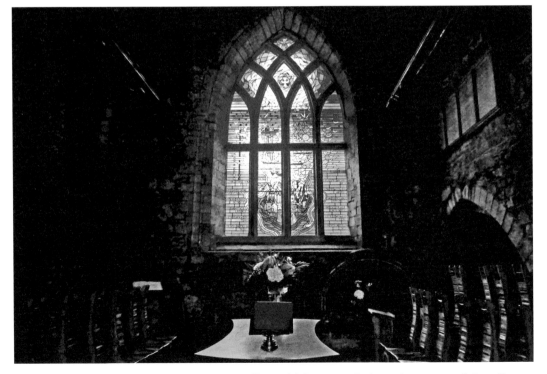

Oil Industry Chapel stained-glass window by Shona McInnes symbolises the impact of the oil industry on Aberdeen. It was dedicated in 1989. (Courtesy of St John's Chapel at the Kirk of St Nicholas Uniting)

The world of work has provided us with its own distinctive vocabulary that can be broken down by dialect. The Doric of north-east Scotland is rich in work-associated terms: yokin-time, when beasts are harnessed at the start of a day's labour; darg is the daily grind, which, if exhausting, is a tyauve; weel vrocht is a job well-done, especially tilling the land; lousin-time marked the end of the day when horse harnesses were removed; an exhausted labourer could be foonert, wabbit, forfochen or, if completely drained, caad deen. Those in cerebral occupations were lang-nibbit – their noses in books.

Over the past 200 years people have been faced with the necessity of finding paid employment – survival in an economy dominated by buying and selling in increasingly national and international markets.

Working lives are further split along lines of class and gender. Female labour, including un-waged running a home and raising a family, has often been seen as inferior to men's daily tyauve.

Aberdeen, a 'market town that is called Apardjon', was by the late Middle Ages one of the four wealthiest burghs in Scotland. Craft skills were honed by people with a reputation for being reserved, who held education in high regard and had 'a bent for minute, detailed work; for accuracy in small things'. This is a story of the women, men and children whose skills, sweat, invention and sometimes the sacrifice of their very lives shaped the economy and appearance of the city of Aberdeen.

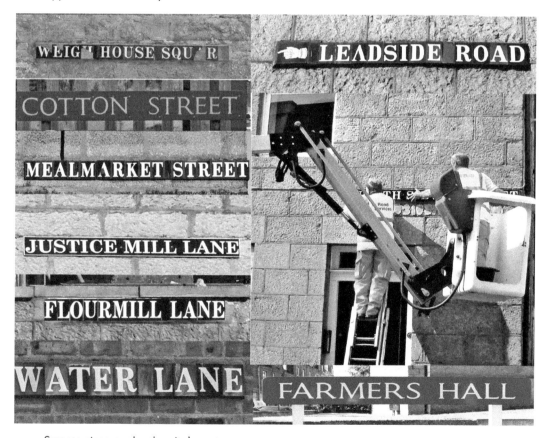

Streets signs evoke the city's past.

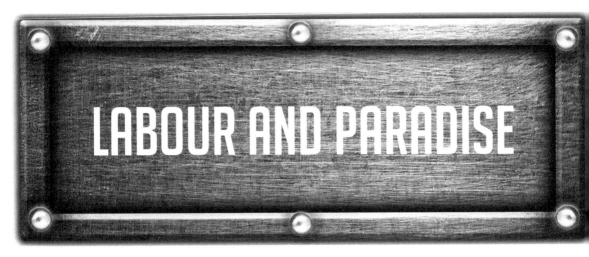

LABOUR AND PARADISE

O ver millennia humankind has sought to alleviate the sheer grinding effort of some tasks using levers, rollers and cranes to manipulate otherwise immoveable objects. Invention and imagination have been essential components of coping with work, but, as the Creation myth of Christianity testifies, coping can be a 'spiritual' exercise rather than a technical fix.

When Adam and Eve were expelled from Paradise it was to face a hostile world; the daily bread had to be earned through labour. Alexander Robb, Aberdeen craft tailor and poet wrote of Paradise, in which Adam could survive without work:

> The luscious fruit o' various kinds,
> Drapt in his mou, like heavenly manna
> An' he could raise his crap o' greens
> Without lime, sharn, or guano.

Sin and the will of God, however, put a stop to the easy life and the unhappy couple and their progeny were compelled,

> To till the grun, that now was curs't
> Wi' thorns, an' briars, an' burry thistles.

The expulsion meant humans being forced to look to their wits to survive. In effect humankind itself became creator, powered by necessity and imagination:

> 'Twas this ca'd forth the arts o' man
> To manufacture ploughs and harrows
> 'Twas then dunghills first began,
> An' spades, and' rakes, an' carts, an' barrows.

Robb is no Milton, but his verse grasps the Christian notion of work based on sin. Another Aberdeen poet, James Ogg, urged labourers not to be downcast. In his *Song for the Workers* he praises their dignity and readiness to get their hands dirty:

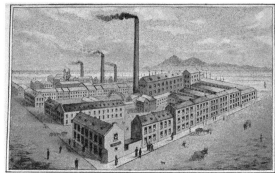

MOIR'S PRESERVED PROVISION FACTORY, ABERDEEN, SCOTLAND.
ESTABLISHED 1822.

John Moir's company near the harbour exported pickles, soups and tinned fish to Britain's colonies.

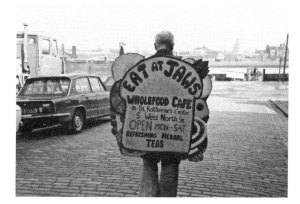

Vegetarian food at Aberdeen's Jaws café, 1970s.

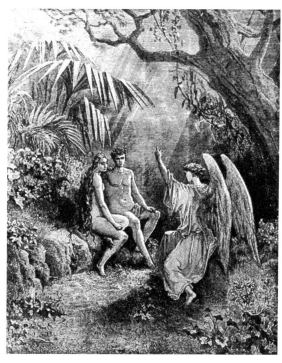

Adam and Eve in Paradise (after Gustave Doré).

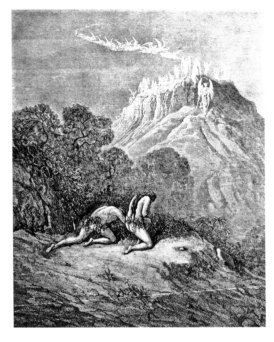

Adam and Eve expelled from Paradise
(after Gustave Doré).

Ay, labour, my lads, is the salt of the earth:
There's nothing of value, there's nothing of worth
But what's been anointed, baptised with oil
Of mental endeavour and physical toil.

Aberdonians, like others, were left to wonder if, short of death and entry to Paradise, would there ever be escape from work's drudgery to a system that was fairer with equitable distribution of toil and wealth?

Shoemaker poet David Wright, a contemporary of Alexander Robb, had an answer. He pointed to the 'charter' with its pledge to democracy as working men's way forward; unity of labour, unity of purpose would make working lives easier. There was no need to wait for the hereafter:

Come then arise-for once be wise.
And imitate the bees;
And all unite in Freedom's fight.
And spoil the sons of ease.

In the event the charter of the 1830s to 1850s failed and working men and women continued to rely on their ability to organise, not forgetting the contribution of the wealth creating dynamics of industrial capitalism.

Aberdonian J. Maclaren Cobban tackled the issue of how to improve the lives of working people in his 1895 novel *The King of Andaman: A Saviour of Society*, a tale of defeated Chartist weavers of 'Ilkastane' (Aberdeen's Gilcomston). Cobban's characters spoke of the folly of dependence on the goodwill of social superiors – 'the excellent public who paid rates and taxes, who had clothes to their back, food for their belly, and money in their purse' – they

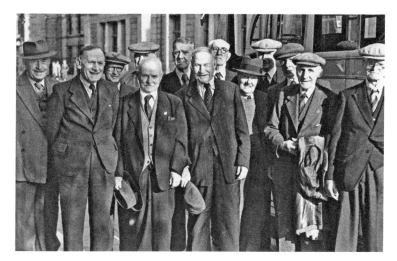

Outing of the Scottish Society of Painters, possibly 1950s; their association badges are prominent on their lapels. William Lyall Smith, third left, is in the bunnet he always wore. (Courtesy of Alan Robertson)

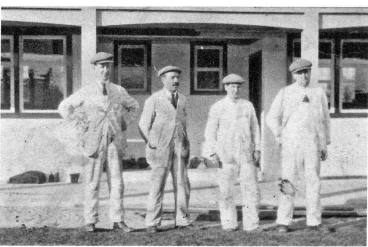

Painters at Hazlehead Golf Pavilion *c.* 1927. Second from right is William Lyall Smith, a foreman painter with the council. He was involved in painting the new houses at Hilton in the 1930s. (Courtesy of Alan Robertson)

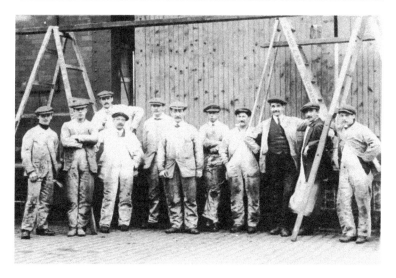

J. Mason & Son, painters, glaziers and paperhangers of Queen Street, at the Fish Market. Robert William Smith, fourth from right, is smoking a clay doddie; his son William Lyall is first on the right. (Courtesy of Alan Robertson)

could only be relied upon to turn disruptive men over to the law. Neither was technology the solution, for it destroyed the handloom weavers. Maclaren Cobban's fictional key to lifting weavers out of their miserable lives was through solidarity and leaving Aberdeen to discover their Eden in the far-off Andaman Islands where families 'could lie in the rustling shade of trees and eat the fruit that drops into your hand and that dissolves in your mouth like ambrosia, the food of the gods'. Alas, this Paradise, promised by O'Rhea, a former militant Chartist, was a chimera calculated to rob the people of the little they had. And so, it would seem, the 'curse' of work is humankind's burden – that might be eased but not abolished.

At a more mundane level improvements to the lot of humble Aberdonian shopworkers came not from any promised New Jerusalem but the introduction of 'Early Closing' at their workplaces. In 1846 shop workers united over the 'pernicious and hurtful' conditions they endured from 'keen and severe' retail competition. Shopworkers, who were overwhelmingly male, enjoyed middle-class support from such as Provost Blaikie and textile manufacturer James Hadden; although the latter while favouring easing life for shop men would not countenance the same for his female mill labourers.

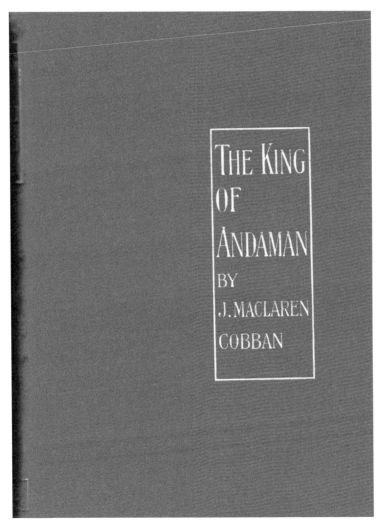

Title cover of the 1895 novel *The King of Andaman*.

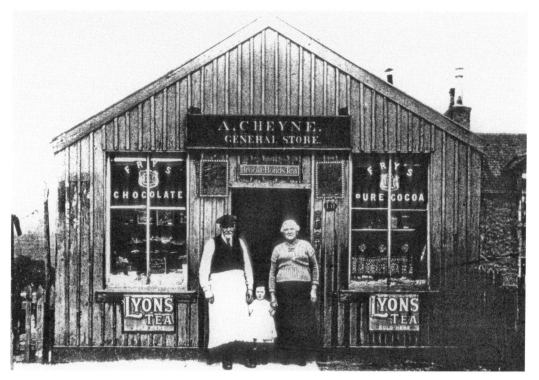

Alexander Cheyne and Catherine Hird at their general store in Woodside. Alexander's family owned chip shops and ran Cheyne's Rooms on Great Northern Road. (Courtesy of Heather Downer)

Shop assistants appealed to middle-class women, asking that their servants should collect purchases by 8 p.m. to give workers time for intellectual and moral improvement. This appeal met with some success. By the end of 1847, with some exceptions, it was granted. 'For the unanimity of feeling which prevailed on the subject, we felt truly grateful, and fondly hoped that, having attained our object, all cause for further agitation had ceased to exist.'

However, there was a sting in the tail for as much as middle-class support was forthcoming the drive of competition remained:

> But we despair of success, even for the most limited period, so long as a class exist where feelings no appeal of a philanthropic character ever warmed, and who thoughtless of the consequences of the system they are perpetrating, never dream that the youth who serve them ever feel fatigue, or that they have minds capable of expansion, by the interchange of ideas round the domestic hearth.

Contrast this with the actions of women and girls employed at Broadford mill who went on strike in 1834 because they 'would no longer submit to oppression and low wages' and who called 'upon their sisters in all the factories in the town to join them'. This kind of militancy was deprecated by James Hadden.

Expulsion from the Garden of Eden led to labour being regarded both as punishment and a means of redemption and signalled that idle hands were dangerous as they might seize what was not theirs and give nothing in return. During the 1730s Aberdeen's civic and ecclesiastical leaders tackled this issue. Aberdeen's streets were filled with 'great numbers of idle people, strolling beggars, and vagabonds'. They were to be taken and placed in what we might now call secure and productive accommodation: a Poors' Hospital or Workhouse. By 1742 provision had been made to house forty men and women, twenty-five boys and thirteen girls and in exchange they would work at the likes of stocking knitting, spinning and what was called 'rasping wood'.

How effective such institutions were on the inmates' moral character is not recorded but in the 1830s Aberdeen's manufacturers in evidence to Parliamentary Commissioners said that children trained to labour made the best workers – best disciplined and best fitted to machine production.

John Milne was six years old when in 1798 he entered the Poors' Hospital. He was put to work 'teazing oakum' and given a modicum of education with daily prayers. Milne recorded how a coterie of boys was so disruptive to the smooth running of the institution its directors resolved to settle residents in apprenticeships by the age of fourteen. John Milne himself left the Poors' Hospital aged twelve in 1803 to begin a six-year apprenticeship as a shoemaker. Another young shoemaker, a generation later, was Thomas Edward who started work at eleven years of age. His day stretched from 6 a.m. to 9 p.m. with two hours allowed for meals. As was common he was subjected to beatings by his master. For the majority whose efforts underpinned the wealth of the town working life was a struggle to be endured driven by necessity.

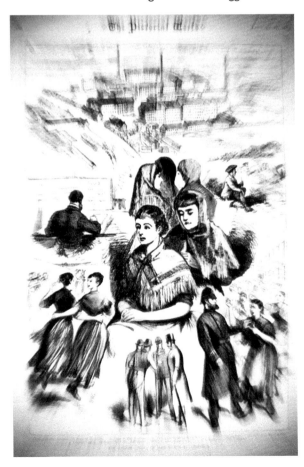

Women's strike, Broadford's.

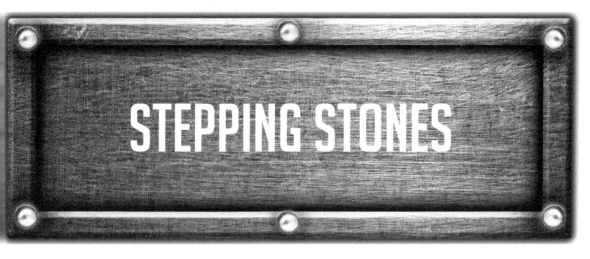

STEPPING STONES

The port of Aberdeen on the edge of what came to be called the North Sea has enjoyed 1,000 years of trade with Europe and the larger world. Close to the city is a spectacular legacy of stone circles constructed through the impressive efforts of our Bronze Age antecedents who collected and worked stone 5,000 years BC. Their achievements were echoed thousands of years later when Aberdeenshire granite was excavated – less for spiritual than commercial purposes. Wool spun and cloth woven by the area's early settlers also began a craft that grew into an enormous industry in Aberdeen. The food fished and farmed and the forests worked and cropped established other occupations and trades for succeeding generations.

Aberdeen and the north-east's abundance of stone including granites and gneisses have been famously exploited for ritual circles, pictorial stones, ornaments and buildings. Stone has been used to transform the landscape: dramatic recumbent stone circles, unique to the north-east; the magnificent granite structures of St Machar's Cathedral and St Nicholas Kirk; and the creation of the Granite City, Aberdeen.

Author Lewis Grassic Gibbon called the monolithic stone circles 'Devil Stones' managed by 'priestly overlords'. His claim that early settlers were 'free and happy ... the world in the

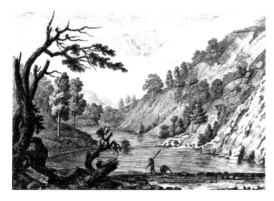

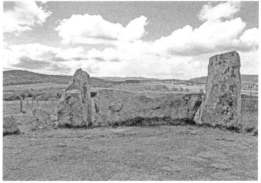

Above left: Early dwellers in the north-east.

Above right: Tomnaverie recumbent stone circle, Tarland, looking towards Lochnagar.

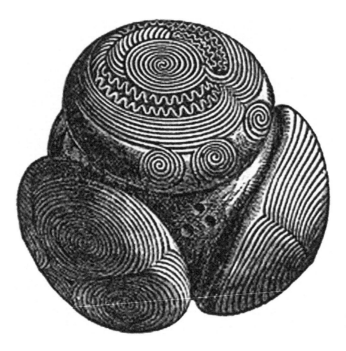

Carved stone ball found at
Towie on Donside.

Golden Age' is questionable but what is not is the effort and energy that went into erecting
the massive circles, which could only have been achieved through the combined endeavours
of communities. We cannot know if the circle-builders' labour was forced or freely given, or
was an obligation to the collective good. Nor do we know if women, men and children were
involved. Was there cooperation between communities sharing labour and knowledge both
symbolic and practical? Did builders interrupt their back-breaking tasks to attend to other
needs such as obtaining food and raising crops?

The sheer volume of stone manipulated meant the work was arduous and dangerous;
operating rollers and levers and coping with the sheer exhaustion of dragging and lifting
immense stones in addition to clearing miles of forest and rough ground to erection sites.
Any dressing of those monoliths was minimal, mainly to keep them standing, although some
stones were decorated with markings – most commonly cup-marks. We can speculate as
to the purpose of the stones, but their positioning implies association with summer and
winter solstices and phases of the moon. Current scholarly thought suggests recumbent
circles were portals between spheres of existence, which takes us back to Grassic Gibbon's
priestly overlord class and whether early communities differentiated between spiritual and
physical labour.

Aside from clearly ceremonial uses of stone the north-east retains evidence of its practical
application among prehistoric peoples. Stone cairns and souterrains or earth houses are
underground chambers thought to have been grain stores; for example, not far from Aberdeen
is the Culsh stone-lined souterrain whose passage broadens at the rear. Carved into the
stone are cup-marks, which might signify units of measurement. Souterrains are sophisticated
examples of building with stone. Construction required cooperation similar to farming as well
as command of how stone can be obtained and dressed to fit a designed space.

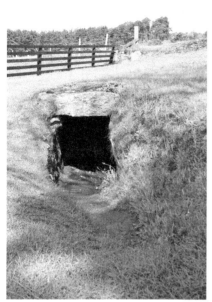

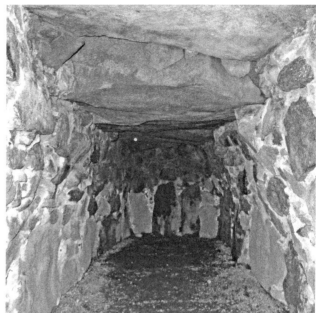

Above left: Entrance to Culsh souterrain.

Above right: Passageway in Culsh souterrain.

Picture stones carved by our Pict ancestors some 3,000 years after the circle builders are equally mysterious to us, but we can admire the skills that went into cutting intricate designs in granite, gneiss and whinstone. Iconography changed when the Picts became Christian and incorporated the cross. The level of proficiency of their stone cutting suggests communities operated divisions of labour including trained masons although not as yet wage earners in a market economy, unlike their nineteenth-century counterparts.

Stones that provided symbolism and shelter for millennia of people were a nuisance to farmers, particularly so when land had to be cleared to grow marketable crops in the 'Age of Improvement' when capitalist farming became ever more important. So much rock was being dug out of the earth that in 1810 one observer described improvers as 'stony-culturists'. Vast quantities were used to make bulwarks, cairns and immense drystane dykes providing the north-east with yet more stone iconography.

What is now Altens on the southern edge of Aberdeen was until recently rough muir and run-rigs. When manual attempts to ply heavy oak and iron levers failed to shift muckle earth-fast boulders, the stones were blown up. Many boulders went into consumption dykes sometime 5 feet tall and 10 feet wide. Smaller stones were used to line the many drainage channels that criss-crossed the muir to make it suitable for farming and housing. Grass divets were mixed with night soil (human waste) from the town, along with huge quantities of whale blubber to make compost for enriching the soil. Men hired for this back-breaking work were paid little and encouraged to stay with generous supplies of alcohol and entertainment.

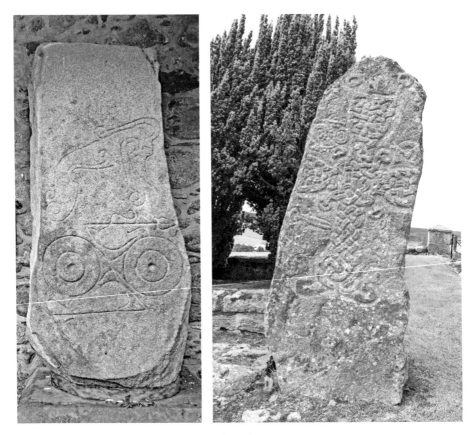

Above left: Pictish symbol stone, Dyce kirkyard.

Above right: Migvie Pict cross slab.

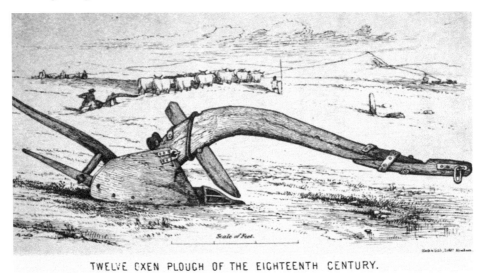

TWELVE CXEN PLOUGH OF THE EIGHTEENTH CENTURY.

Working unimproved land with a 'primitive' plough.

The town's food came mainly from the surrounding countryside where semi-subsistence agriculture gave way to capital invested in land and wage labour. Male farmhands were housed in either bothies or chaumers. Bothies were small buildings where unmarried men provided for themselves while chaumers were commonly loft spaces in farmhouses and men lodged in them shared the farmer's family table. The relative freedom of the bothy was criticised for breeding loose morals and much condemned by churchmen.

Labourers moved from farm to farm, their movement controlled by law through the Master and Servant Act. Twice yearly at feeing markets men and women gathered to meet and bargain their hire and wages with local farmers. 'Muckle Fridays' at Whitsun and Martinmas provided rare relief from the grind of agricultural toil. Drams, conviviality and drunkenness abounded to an extent that shocked local burghers and churchmen alike who condemned feeing markets for encouraging depravity. A formal registration system, with ministers vouching for the moral rectitude of labourers, was suggested but came to nothing. A newspaper correspondent calling himself 'Ploughman' argued that only better working and living conditions would remove the explosive joys of feeing markets: 'Give us houses, and homes, that we may enjoy the comforts of a civilised state of society, and we will not be the care-for-nothing semi-barbarians that we are now said to be.'

In 1848 'Johnny Raw' defended rural labour. Castigating narrow-mindedness he asked if Aberdeen's good citizens expected men 'to live like earth moles ... deprived of the right to ... glorious ... comradeship and be no happier than an ill-greased threshing mill'. Feeing markets, he said, encouraged a 'spirit of "intermixture"'.

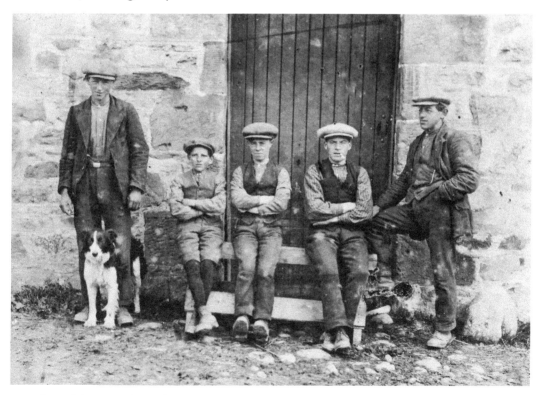

Farm labourers from the period of the bothy system – note the very young boys, better known locally as 'halflins'. (Courtesy of Professor Paul Dukes)

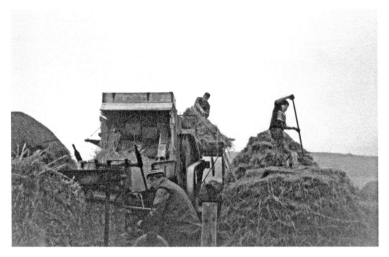

Demonstration of a thrashing mill at work, 1990s.

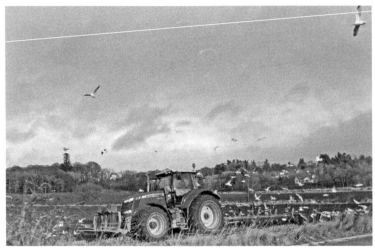

As much as Aberdeen is seen as the oil capital of Europe, it retains a close connection with agriculture. Ploughing the land is still seen within the city limits in the twenty-first century.

In 1849 Aberdeen Town Council attempted to tackle the so-called nuisance by moving the feeing market from its conspicuous site on King Street. Their alternative was the old Poultry Market, but it proved too small and cramped and both farmhands and farmers defiantly returned to King Street. The council tried to get them to meet at the Links, even farther out of town, but faced with more opposition relented and agreed to Castle Street's use. It must have been a squeeze, for in 1860 some 4,000 gathered to find a fee and enjoy the pleasures of company.

Aberdeen developed around the mouth of the River Dee, shore, the Green and Castlegate, with expansion coming in fits and starts, resulting in its population living cheek by jowl. Gardens of large town properties were subdivided into lanes and pends crammed with dwellings. The sea made eastward expansion impossible, so the town stretched north, west and south, eventually swallowing up private estates and villages such as Rubislaw and Woodside. With growth came improved road access, which involved bridging the rivers Dee and Don.

Access to southern markets came via the imposing 1527 Bridge of Dee built under James V's mason Thomas Franche (his name suggests his roots were French) who also worked on

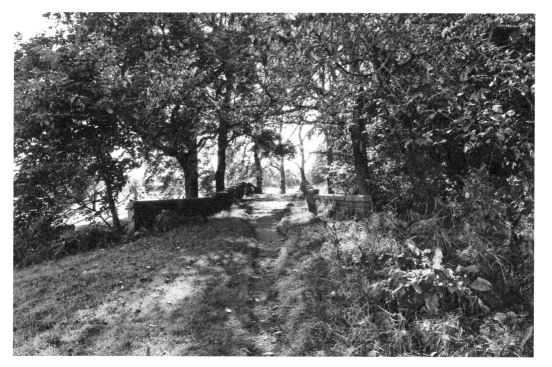

Packhorse brig over the River Dee, removed to Riverside. The parapet was added in 1923.

St Machar's Cathedral and cut the original stone crown decorating King's College. Smaller packhorse brigs were used by merchants such George Davidson of Pattens who from humble beginnings went on to amass a fortune and became a town burgess. Some of his wealth was shared with local kirks: Newhills, Fittie and St Nicholas – where he lies buried.

Entry to and from the north was improved when a thoroughfare was ploughed between Aberdeen and Inverurie close to the Hadagain (no 'u' in the old spelling) Inn and smithy at Woodside. Later a canal was dug for easier transportation of goods and animals between Aberdeen harbour and Port Elphinstone. The 1807 24-foot-wide canal entailed seventeen locks, fifty-six bridges, five aqueducts and twenty culverts. The £38,000 outlay came from public subscription. The *Countess of Kintore*, with a gun at her prow, was the first barge to complete the 18 miles. She did it in seven and half hours; slower than travel along the turnpike road, but possibly the cattle on board did not mind. Barge passengers were charged 2d per mile or 2s for the complete journey. Locals used the frozen canal for skating in cold winters and bathing in summer and when the railway company GNSR forced its closure in 1854 Woodside villagers were compensated for loss of their water source with a payment of £1,000.

Impressive as standing stones and circles are around Aberdeen, they are dwarfed in output terms by the volume and variety of the area's once great granite industry. It was in the 1760s that a near insatiable demand for road stone prompted the production of Aberdeen cassies. Quarrymen in town and shire extracted granite by the thousands of tons for dressing and shipment to London and other commercial centres. The trade depended upon manual labour and years of collective experience in working the obdurate stone. With the introduction of technology more complex and ornate working was made possible. Aberdeen became the centre of Britain's granite trade.

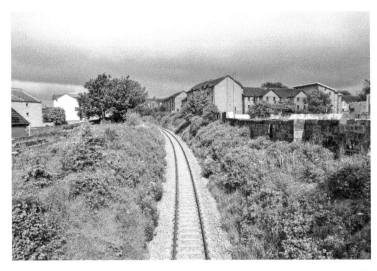 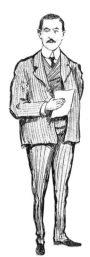

Above left: Waterloo station to Kittybrewster rail line, seen from Constitution Street – originally the Aberdeen Canal.

Above right: George Davidson, general manager of the Great North of Scotland Railway, early twentieth century.

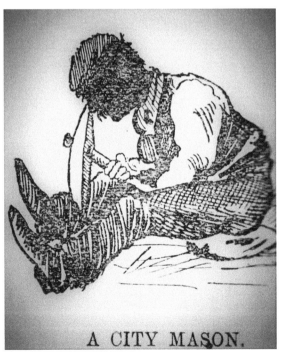 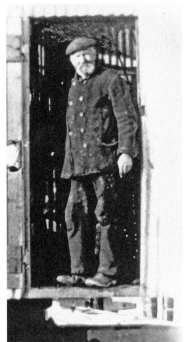

Above left: Silhouette of granite mason with pick.

Above right: William Cheyne beside his blondin (cableway), probably at Sclattie quarry c. 1910–20. (Courtesy of Heather Downer, his great-granddaughter)

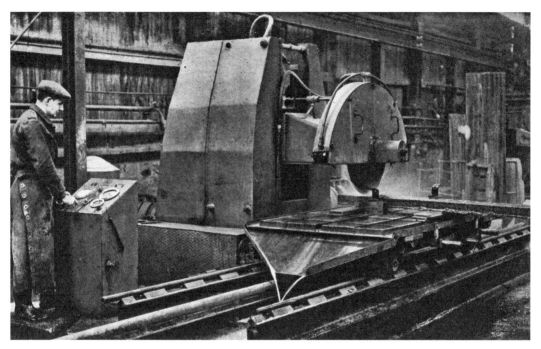

Cutting granite with circular carbo-saw.

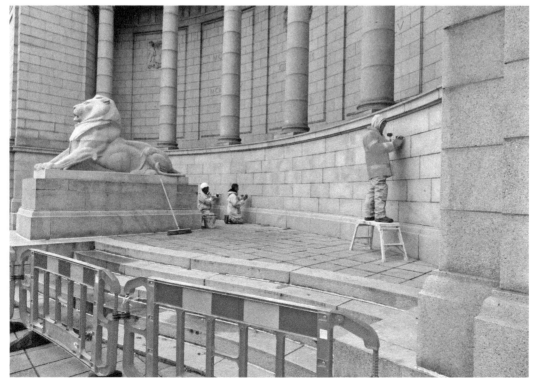

Masons giving a tidy up to stonework at Aberdeen's war memorial, 2014.

The end of the eighteenth century witnessed an escalation in imposing domestic and commercial architecture. Common rubble-building gave way to beautifully dressed ashlar. Granite offered colour variations from light greys and blues to pinks and reds providing architects with opportunities to generate flamboyance without time-consuming ornamental carving. In the 1830s handling of stone was transformed when Alexander Macdonald introduced steam power to drive saws, lathes and polishing mills.

Aberdeen's granite industry was characterised by an accumulation of small work yards producing stone for one-off customers, with much of their livelihood coming from memorial production. As the city prospered and production costs fell the market for carved granite slabs increased. A few stoneyards were distinguished by their high level of mechanisation, although hand cutting and carving remained at the heart of their work. With its flourishing local, national and international economy Aberdeen was regarded as the 'Granite City'.

Change arrived. The US market, which had been very important, was undermined by the expansion of America's own industry, increasingly safeguarded by import tariffs. America's granite trade was partly built on skills and knowledge imported from Aberdeen and it enjoyed the advantages of sheer scale and technological dynamism. Its success dealt a blow to Aberdeen's merchants.

By the mid-twentieth century Aberdeen's granite dominance was all but a memory. The trade continued but its international importance was diminished, as was granite's significance in the town's economy. Closures, rationalisation and merging of companies attempted to safeguard the industry but to little avail. Symbolic of the industry's decline was the closure of Rubislaw Quarry in 1971, which had been worked since the early eighteenth century. Over 400 feet deep – spectacular but an uneconomic headache for quarriers – the quarry's demise underlined the general state of the granite trade. Stone is still worked in the city, employing sophisticated technology along with traditional methods of working, but is a marginal trade.

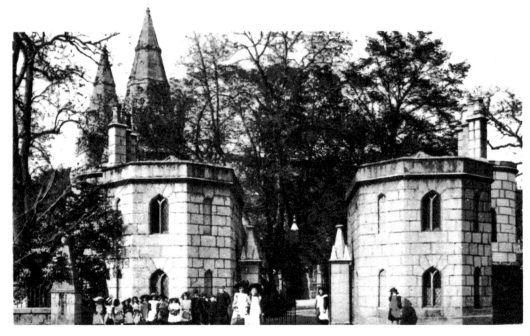

Children and teacher at the gates of the granite St Machar's Cathedral.

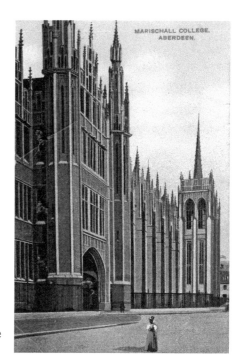

Façade of Marischal College, an ornate granite triumph. This Gothic-inspired work gave aesthetic voice to architect Alexander Marshall Mackenzie and pays homage to the skills of the Granite City's masons.

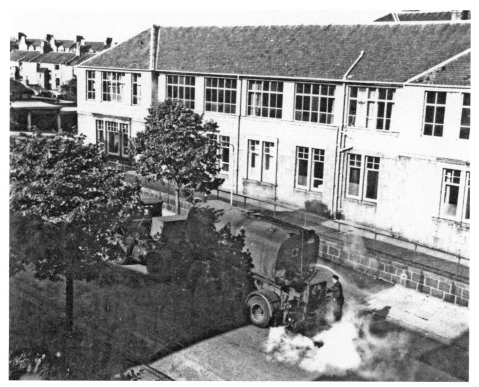

Surfacing Grampian Road, Torry, 1970s. Tarmacadam, quieter than cassies, killed off older skills of the granite trade.

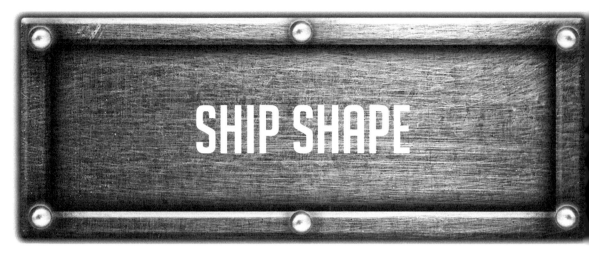

SHIP SHAPE

Exclusive arrangements between the town's early wealthy merchant burgesses and the Crown conferred their right to hold markets, and control the quality, quantity, display and sale of commodities. A surviving royal charter of 1180 that records the arrangement by which the port of Aberdeen could lawfully trade with Continental Europe was the start of a lang sang that is still being sung. Merchant ships frequently carried fish (chiefly salmon), wool, hides and furs to foreign markets, mainly Baltic and the Low Countries, and brought back all types of goods – principally wine, crockery and timber. Seven hundred years later leading exports were granite, grain and oatmeal; linen, cotton and woollen items; cattle, sheep and swine; timber; dairy products; preserved foods; and yet more salmon. Key imports comprised coal, lime, bones, iron, wheat, hemp, jute and guano.

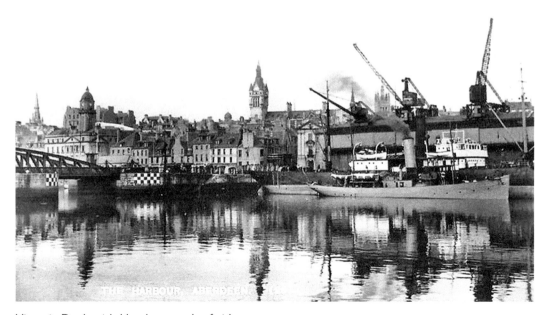

Victoria Dock with Henderson wharf-side cranes.

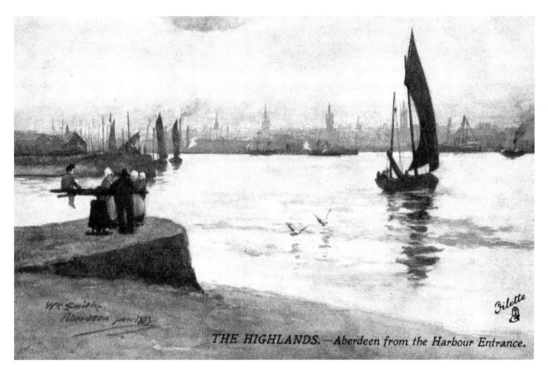

THE HIGHLANDS.—*Aberdeen from the Harbour Entrance.*

At the capstan – south shore of the harbour entrance.

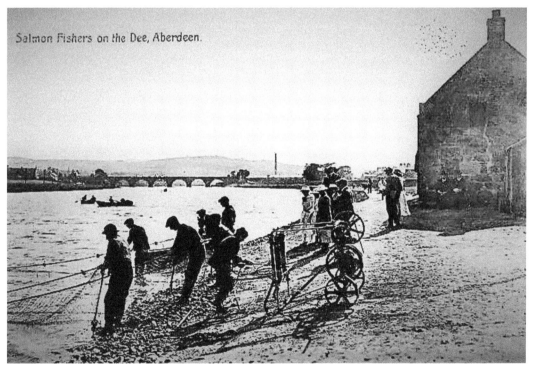

Salmon Fishers on the Dee, Aberdeen.

Fishing next to the salmon fishers' bothy at the Dee.

Aberdeen was Scotland's biggest and most important port. With so much wealth tied up in its merchant shipping, royal vessels provided protection against pirates and 'alagards'. This constant threat was taken very seriously by merchants whose livelihoods depended on imports and exports.

Non-burgess craftsmen had restrictions imposed on sales of their goods at home markets and similarly non-burgh merchants were obliged to pay higher duties – 'hostiliagium' – to the monarch to participate in overseas trade. Regulations were tight with checks made for quality, weight and the application of duties. In Scotland the tax point was known as the Tron, hence Trongate, but in Aberdeen it was always called the Weighhouse.

PYNOURS

We know from Aberdeen's burgh registers of the 1540s that the city's pynours were tasked with keeping the harbour area clean and tidy. 'The pynouris to help to dycht & cleynge the calsais, euery pynours his day abowtt. Small expensis and wncostisis sic as keill hyiris, pynours feis, walking on the [quay] heid.'

This was not the earliest evidence of the pynours or Shore Porters. Burgh records of 1498 describe their dress: corduroy trousers and sturdy, blue, pilot swallow-tailed coats with brass buttons. It is thought the pynours have been in existence since at least the 1200s when Aberdeen's trading links with the Continent were starting to thrive.

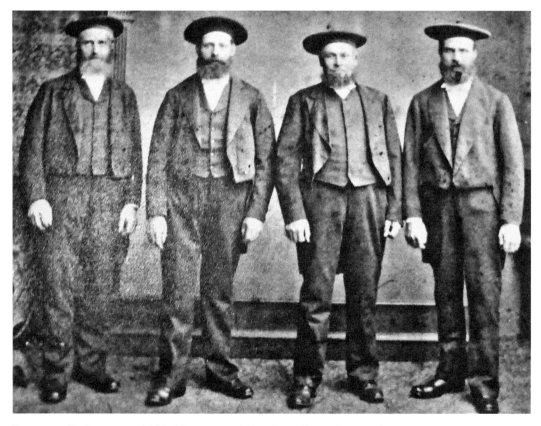

Pynour coffin bearers, *c.* 1880. (Courtesy of Aberdeen Shore Porters Society)

Pynours originally were recruited from Futty's fishing community, whose livelihoods depended on the water but their strange name is thought to have its roots in Middle Dutch. Partly run by the town authorities the Shore Porters only became fully independent as late as 1850.

Women as well as men could be pynours; Megy Tod is listed along with Hungrie Jok and Canny Dog as 'warkwomen' and 'warkmen' who walked gangplanks to load and discharge ships' cargoes. In common with other occupations, fishing communities did not assume women incapable of physical work. For instance, fishermen were carried on their wives' backs out to boats to keep them dry and women traditionally hawked fresh fish packed into heavy wicker creels carried over their backs. However, women's employment as porters faced barriers when in 1636 town magistrates imposed a test of strength for those hoping to become 'shoar porters'. The ordeal comprised carrying a hundredweight load on the back for a mile uphill from the Blockhouse at the harbour to the Braid Gutter in town. Unsurprisingly some women (and some men) found the challenge too arduous and the Futty link was further broken when burlier country loons were recruited.

Pynours literally staggered coping with heavy burdens and sometimes resorted to wheelbarrows – the first recorded use of them in Aberdeen was in 1494 when stone to build King's College was being transported. Goods were moved by the most efficient means – by barrow, sledge, bogie, cart, later motor lorries or simply on the back. The heavily padded coat worn by pynours provided some protection from the awkward, heavy loads they had to carry – a practice known as 'tursing'. Very heavy goods might necessitate a 'twa men's lift' where two pynours walked shoulder to shoulder sharing the weight of the burden attached to a long pole or 'sting' between them.

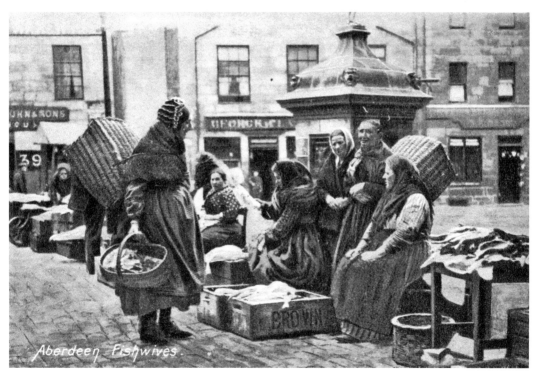

Fishwives in the Green seated by the Mannie Well.

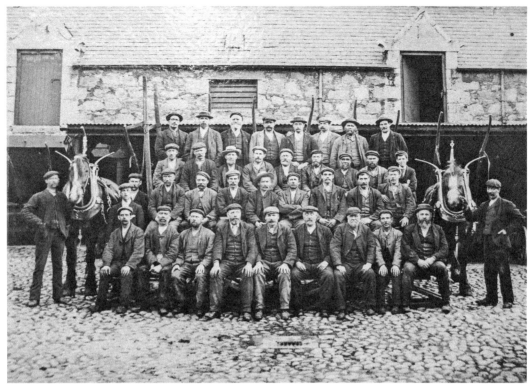

Shore Porters stables at Cotton Street, 1903. (Courtesy of Aberdeen Shore Porters Society)

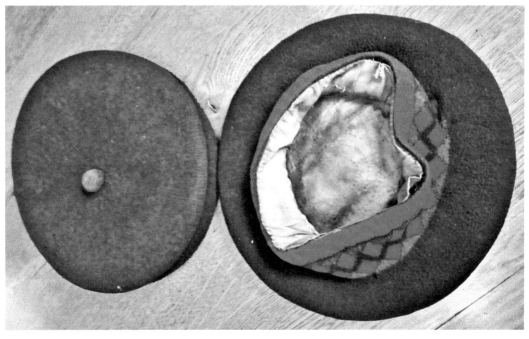

Pynour's traditional woollen bonnets. (Courtesy of Aberdeen Shore Porters Society)

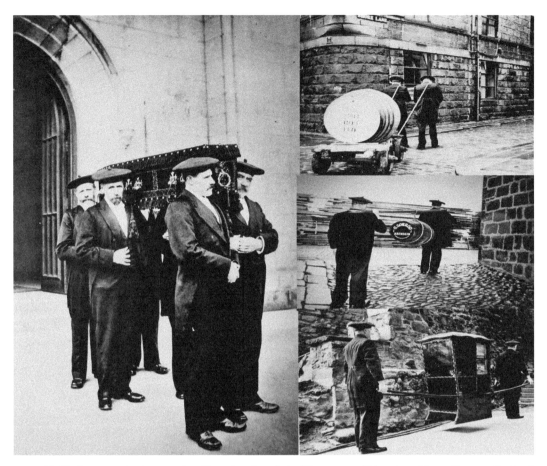

Coffin bearers, the bogey, sting lift and sedan chair. (Courtesy of Aberdeen Shore Porters Society)

In a world of fast-changing events it is extraordinary to note Aberdeen's Shore Porters have been a feature of the city for around a thousand years. They were entrusted with keys to the Weigh-house and Pack-house where linen and other goods were inspected, weighed, packed and stamped 'Insignia Urbis Abredoniae' – the town's official mark of quality.

These brawny individuals were traditionally hired to bear coffins at funerals. In the eighteenth century they bore the living along town streets in sedan chairs and were firefighters. They also moved household goods, and this practice is more familiar to us today under the name Shore Porters. Warkmen or Shore Porters were crucial to the town's mercantile prosperity and enjoyed special privileges such as free drink and salt.

Aberdeen's Shore Porters Society is one of the earliest and surviving co-operative businesses in the UK – sharing profits among members. It has extended into England and operates a fleet of thirty vans and lorries and is itself as international as the trade it enabled through Aberdeen harbour all those centuries ago; yet, with eleven warehouses and its headquarters near the harbour, it has hardly moved location in 1,000 years.

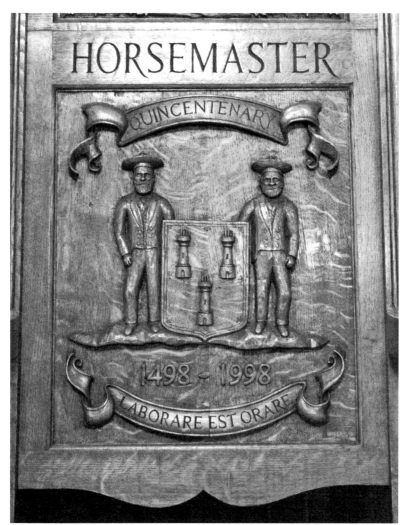

The horsemaster's chair: *laborare est orare* – to work is to pray. The horsemaster in charge of the stables decided journey distances and weights of goods to be moved. (Courtesy of Aberdeen Shore Porters Society)

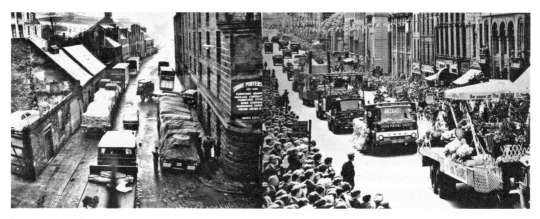

Two images: Shore Porter vehicles at Virginia Street (1975), and decorated floats on parade along Union Street. (Courtesy of Aberdeen Shore Porters Society)

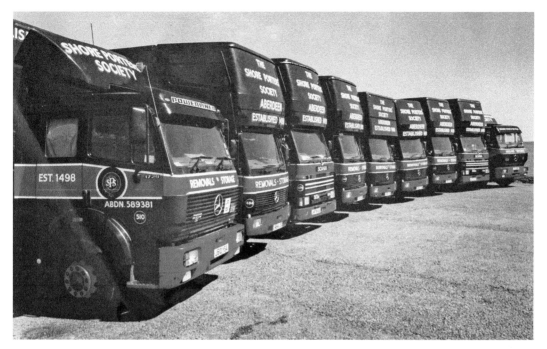

Fleet of Shore Porter vans. (Courtesy of Aberdeen Shore Porters Society)

SHIPBUILDING

Local timber would have been used by Aberdeen's first settlers to build boats to fish out of the Dee, Don and in Aberdeen Bay. When venturing farther afield it was foreign vessels that were used to carry goods in the town's trade with Continental Europe. Tithes from these ships (called 'snows' or 'snauws' because of their snout-like forecastles that better coped with choppy northern waters) went towards upkeep of St Machar's Cathedral.

By the early 1300s and the reign of Robert the Bruce, Scottish boats were beginning to be employed as merchant vessels, and this encouraged shipbuilding. Local linen was still used for sails, but some ship timbers were imported. That said, until the 1700s boatbuilding was a relatively small concern. This is perhaps nicely demonstrated by the struggle of carpenter James Main and his wife when launching the vessel *Maiden of Torry*, which they built on the Torry side of the Dee and involved hauling the boat across ground to the water. A disgruntled town council, who owned the land, refused main permission for a whole year before relenting.

On a far bigger scale Alexander Hall & Co. launched an 82-ton vessel, Ship No. 2 in their register, in 1811, called *Glasgow Packet*. Hall's order book shows how sailing ships became ever larger. The 523-ton *Asia* built for the East India Company was launched in 1819. It proved such a 'prodigy ... people flocked from town and country to see the great ship take to the water'. Its glorious launch, however, was followed by less than glorious charters to carry convicts to Van Diemen's Land. Success for Hall & Co. came with Britain's burgeoning economy and improvements carried out to the harbour by the Council and Harbour Commissioners. Improvements were needed as the harbour was tidal severely limiting maritime traffic. Port reconstruction encouraged shipbuilding and by the 1830s firms such as William Duthie, Walter Hood and John Vernon were competing with Hall for orders.

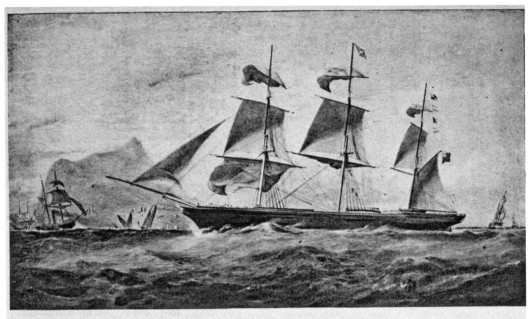

The "Stornoway"

Clipper ship *Stornoway*, built by Alexander Hall and launched in 1850. For a decade she was a swift carrier of tea from the Far East, owned by imperialist trader Jardine Matheson.

Aberdeen's shipyards acquired a reputation for both the quality of timber used and workmanship. The innovation of the Aberdeen Bow which created a sleek cut-away stem improved sailing efficiency. The design retained cargo capacity while reducing duties paid by merchants shipping goods; a canny development from canny Aberdonians. Hall's *Scottish Maid*, launched in 1839 to trade between Aberdeen and London, was the first ship to feature the improved clipper bow.

Clipper ships were timber vessels built using traditional woodworking skills. Aberdeen schooner *Torrington*, operating on the Far East's lucrative opium trade, which brought fortunes for British merchants and misery for others, was a good example. More famous was *Thermopylae*, a latecomer to the clipper class of vessels. Built by Walter Hood's yard for George Thomson's Aberdeen White Star Line in 1868, this iron-framed, wooden-hulled tea clipper covered the distance between Britain and Australia in a record-breaking sixty-three days. Having proved her credentials for speed, essential to Europe's thriving competitive tea market, *Thermopylae* was ideally suited to the Far Eastern trade. Each new tea season was eagerly anticipated by tea importers in expectation of high prices. Sadly for *Thermopylae*, and despite its extreme speed, her entry into the maritime trade coincided with the opening of the Suez Canal, which gradually eliminated the need for long voyages around the Cape of Good Hope. This was also when marine engines were being made more efficient and iron-constructed steam vessels were making their appearance.

Aberdeen had ready access to timber, but needed to import iron and coal so the city's shipyards could adapt to newer types of vessel. *Mercury* of 1840 was an iron schooner built by Blaikie-Duffus. When launched it had to be hauled across a road (echoes of John Mair's difficulty the previous century) and part of a wall at the harbour had to be

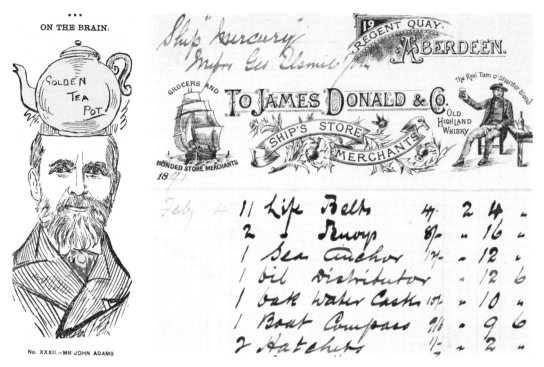

...
ON THE BRAIN.

GOLDEN TEA POT

No. XXXII.—MR JOHN ADAMS

Above left: John Adams, tea importer and taster at No. 64 Green. Tea was sold by the pound or chest.

Above right: Final supplies from James Donald of Aberdeen to doomed schooner *Mercury*, 1891.

demolished. On its entry into the water *Mercury* shot across the harbour smack into the vessel *Sovereign*. An inauspicious start for Mercury, which spent most of the next twenty years carrying coal for brewer and shipowner George Elsmie, before being grounded and lost at the North Pier in 1866.

Significantly, Elsmie chose to replace the lost schooner with a traditional timber-built one. The new *Mercury*, a modest sized ship of 361 tons, was launched in 1871 from Duthie's yard. The ship master was David Thomas. Man and schooner travelled the globe – the Far East, Americas, Australasia and Mediterranean – seeking out profitable cargoes. Merchant voyages were fraught with dangers and exceedingly hard work. *Mercury*'s crews shipped all sorts of goods, some dirty and noxious, e.g. coal to Australia, imported guano from South America, and sulphur from Sicily. Captain and crew spent months at sea with few opportunities to return to Aberdeen, but when they did David Thomas was quick to complain about the hardships he endured coping with poor weather, handling disgruntled crews and meeting delivery deadlines. In a narrative all too familiar, *Mercury* met a sad end: running aground on the Longsand, off Harwich, in March 1891. The crew was saved but ship and cargo were lost.

Into the twentieth century iron-steel vessels were the norm. The famous Duthie shipbuilders did not survive far into this century. Walter Hood & Co. merged with Alex Hall & Co. in 1881. In turn Hall & Co. merged with Aberdeen's last shipbuilders, Hall, Russell & Co., in 1957. Hall, Russell built the Strath class of trawlers – fishing vessels formed a

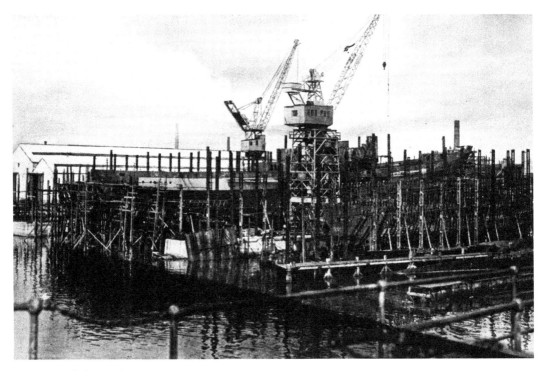

Hall, Russell shipyard.

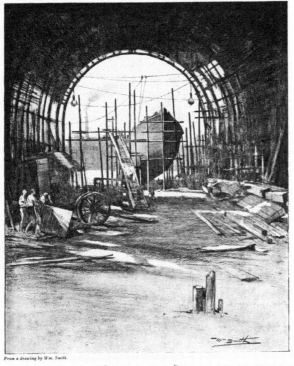

From a drawing by Wm. Smith.

SHIPBUILDING ON THE DEE.

Shipyard.

large part of Aberdeen shipbuilders' work, which also included naval vessels, minesweepers, cargo ships and ferries. John Lewis & Sons was another big name in Aberdeen shipyards. Established in 1907, Lewis' boat construction began in 1917 with wartime demand for coastal vessels. Taken over by the Wood Group in the 1970s, Lewis' closed soon after. Hall, Russell's closure in 1992 brought Aberdeen's long shipbuilding tradition to an end and with it work for the many trades involved in the yards: shipwrights, platers, engineers, carpenters, riveters, welders being a few. International competition and changes in government policy undermined profitability. Hall, Russell's yard became a deepwater berth for vessels employed in Aberdeen's large oil industry.

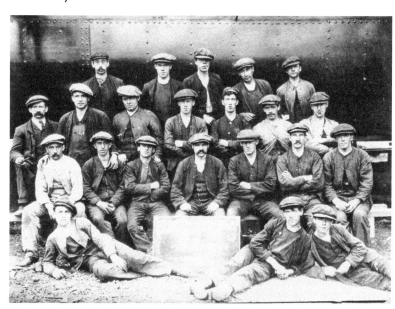

Following his Hall, Russell apprenticeship William Robertson, front third left, looked for work in Govan shipyards and was briefly a ranch hand in Canada. Returning to Aberdeen, he opened his first chip shop in 1933. (Courtesy of Alan Robertson)

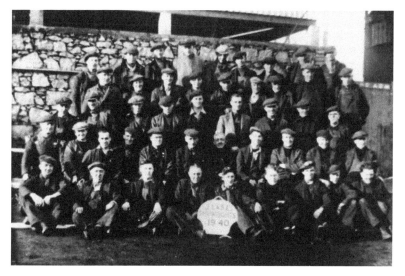

Group of shipwrights employed by John Lewis & Son Ltd, Torry, 1940. William Robertson is first right, row two. (Photo courtesy of his grandson Alan Robertson)

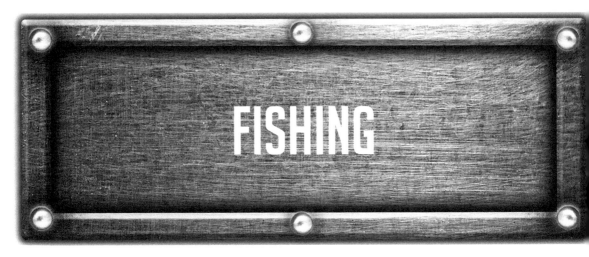

FISHING

Before oil there was fishing. Aberdeen's name was synonymous with fishing, for local consumption and export. Pre-Reformation fishing was carried out every day of the week with Sunday catches called 'holy day's fish', and the tax raised from Sunday fish went towards St Nicholas Kirk's coffers (portions of profits from sales of goods and animals traditionally went to churches).

Torry's devout fisherfolk attended St Fittick's Kirk before Nigg Parish Church opened in 1829. They wore their 'Sunday best' clothes, which for women included a vivid scarlet cloak and tall white cap. On weekdays women as well as men worked at the fish. In their tight-knit communities young and old contributed towards making and repairing nets and lines, collecting bait, setting hooks, cleaning and selling fish. During the three months of the annual herring season entire families moved to wherever herring was being fished and landed. Herring delivered riches for some. In 1878, 93,344 barrels of cured white herring were landed in Aberdeen from a fleet of 374 boats manned by around 1,000 men and boys. In addition to herring tens of thousands of barrels of other species were caught and processed including haddock, halibut, turbot, cod, ling and hake.

The advent of steam trawling led to increased landings of fish, beyond the capacity of the old market at Commercial Quay so a specially designed replacement opened on Market Street in 1889. Feet secured in leather and wooden clogs with copper caps and brass rivets, market porters and lumpers navigated boxes, fish slime and ice in the 3.25 acres of the new market. Aberdeen was Haddockopolis, Scotland's premier white fishing port, so described by the National Sea Fisheries Protection Association in 1905. Around then Aberdeen's annual catch was worth around £800,000 from some 200 trawlers employing over 1,800 men. Around twenty years earlier white fish values stood below £10,000.

As the fishing industry expanded, so too did support services, creating employment for tens of thousands of workers – coopers making barrels, wooden crate makers, curers, processors, shipbuilders and repairers, ice manufacturers and so on.

It was not all success, however. Older fishing communities with traditional sail boats could not compete against the powerful steam trawlers that literally destroyed their inshore fishing grounds. Andrew Walker of Fittie said machinery should be damned as 'manual labour was the best thing in the world and trawling was an abomination and disgust to the sea'.

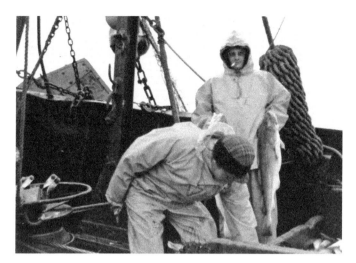

Sorting the catch on deck of the Aberdeen trawler *Strathella, c.* 1980.

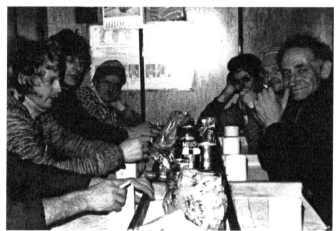

The crew of the *Strathella* rest up between hauls.

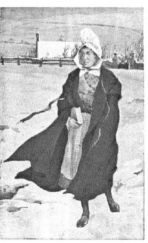

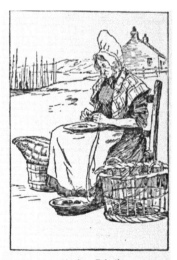

Traditional dress of Aberdeen fishwives.

An Aberdeen Fisher Lass of the Olden Time

Aberdeen Fishwife
Wearing the old Cochernonny Mutch

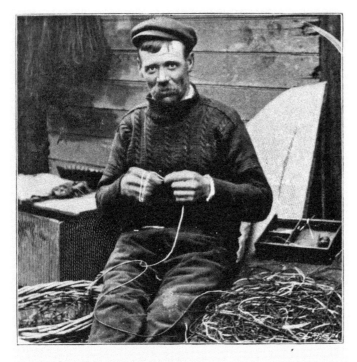

Repairing the lines.

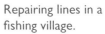

Repairing lines in a fishing village.

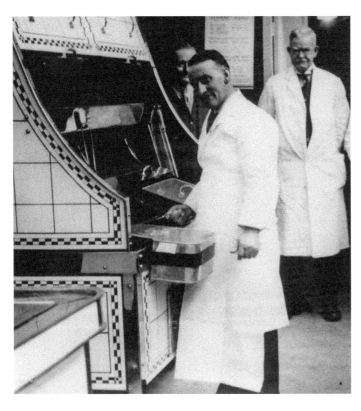

William Robertson at a 1940s trade show. A shipwright by trade, he later owned fish and chip shops and a fish restaurant. (Courtesy of Heather Downer)

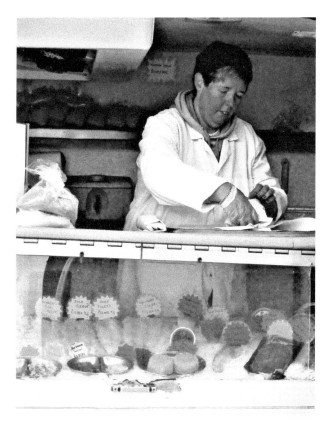

Selling fish around town and county in the twenty-first century. (Courtesy of Jill Thomson)

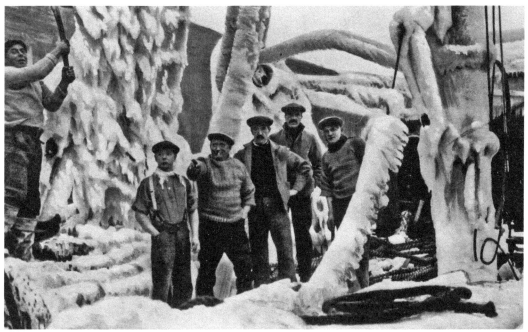

Icing-up of rigging was an occupational hazard during hard winter fishing.

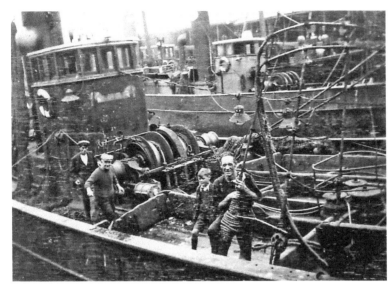

Trawl engineer David Lockhart (right) with his son David, who was lost at sea off Duncansby Head in 1959 when the trawler *George Robb* ran aground. Two months before David Sr was born his father drowned in the Bay of Biscay from SS *Cyenus*, 1882. (Courtesy of Heather Downer)

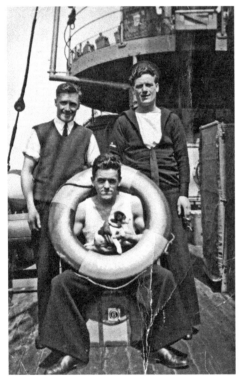

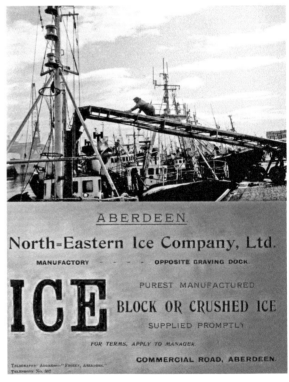

Above left: Alex Dey, left, one of the many Aberdeen trawlermen who enlisted in the Royal Navy in 1939, joining HMT *Warland* in 1940. The ship was sunk in April 1941.

Above right: Gingerly climbing up a conveyor, a worker from the ice factory eases a blockage as a trawler takes on ice before sailing to the fishing grounds. Albert Quay, 1970s.

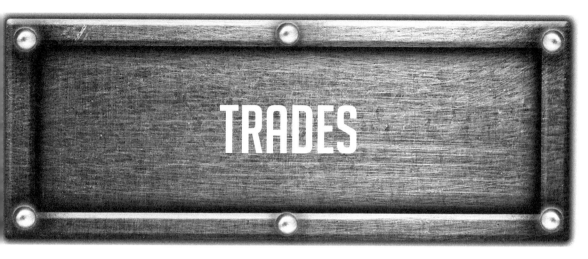

TRADES

The Seven Incorporated Trades of Aberdeen are of great antiquity. The body was established to bring together individual trade guilds for greater protection of their rights and privileges and to impose control over the production and sale of goods locally, including exclusive access of town men to Aberdeen's markets.

The right to form trade guilds and enjoy trading privileges were granted by the Crown to Aberdeen's burgesses as long ago as the twelfth century, but it was only in the summer of 1587 at a meeting of craftsmen guilds that a Common Indenture, sometimes described as Aberdeen's Magna Carta, was drawn up. This combined Trades body was expected to

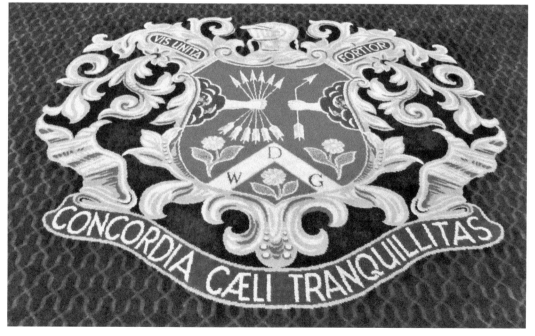

The crest of the Seven Incorporated Trades of Aberdeen includes six good arrows signifying collective strength, with a broken one representing weakness.

resolve disputes between merchant and craft burgesses and unfair practices within trades. An example from the 1490s involved Sandy Kemp, who was accused of 'hindering the proffeitt' of his fellow baxters (bakers) by undermining their prices.

Trade disputes were heard by the Deacon Convener or Master of Trade. The first recorded Deacon Convener is in June 1587 with the appointment of saddler, George Elphinstone, a member of the guild of Hammermen.

The so-called protections offered by the Trades could prove irksome to those being criticised, such as mid-seventeenth-century coopers accused of selling poor quality casks to the salmon trade that 'spill the pickle and so the salmon are spoillit'. The Trades controlled pricing, part of what's been called a 'moral economy', a means of ensuring a degree of social harmony to protect the poor and others from sharp practices. In 1584 the town council found wabsters (weavers) guilty of overcharging, for the 'gryt and exorbitant pryces taken be thame for the weyving of all soirtis of claytht'.

As well as looking after its individual bodies the Incorporated Trades provided help for members too old or too infirm to work. Prior to the twentieth century there were no pensions in the United Kingdom for the frail and elderly. Small charity handouts might be available otherwise families, often poor themselves, carried full responsibility for each other. In Aberdeen, St Thomas' Hospital was a sanctuary for craft burgesses no longer able to work until the council forced their exclusion in 1609. Up stepped Dr William Guild, principal of King's College. This son of a wealthy 'swerd slipper' or armourer provided the Trades with their own headquarters near the Green – a former monastery belonging to the Red Friars of the Holy Trinity. This roomy accommodation doubled as a meeting place and hospital (in the old sense) for burgess tradesmen who were sober and devout. Too sober and devout it happened, for many of the town's old craftsmen who turned their backs on charity with

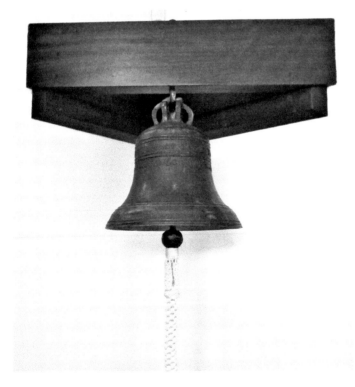

The Trades' ancient bell used to summon members of the Incorporation to meetings and meals.

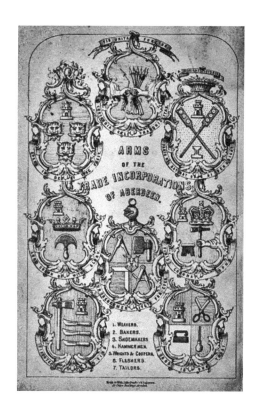

Arms of the Trades.

strings attached. By 1771 the Trades were investing in property to provide for a members' widow fund, now a highly valuable asset, and in 1803 the Trades began distributing pensions to its members.

In 1845 the Seven Incorporated Trades moved from the Green to Union Street and moved again in the 1960s to their present home on Holburn Street. Preserved at each address is their association with the Red Trinity Friars – hence their hall is always the Trinity Hall or Ha'.

Let us take a closer look at those trades within the Incorporated Trades in part through the Ha's impressive artefacts, including the Trinity Ha's magnificent collection of chairs ('cheers' in Doric) presented by each of the trades, some of the fine painted coats of arms that represent the old guilds and essay or test pieces submitted by aspiring members who must satisfy their membership suitability through a sample of work.

A recurring emblem evident in the Ha' are seven arrows: six whole and one broken, signifying strength that underpinned the formation of the Incorporated Trades.

Hammermen's status as the pre-eminent of the seven trades presumably derives from its role making swords and armour for wealthy and influential individuals. Other metal crafts that come under the umbrella of hammermen, in addition to sword slippers and armourers, are cutlers, glaziers, pewterers, glovers, goldsmiths, blacksmiths, gunsmiths, saddlers and hookmakers. Hammermen were incorporated in 1519.

Wrights and Coopers incorporated in 1527 embraced timber-based occupations such as cartwrights, wheelwrights, housewrights (carpenters), cabinetmakers, woodcarvers and coopers (whose barrels were used to store everything from food and drink to dry goods) and for a time included masons. This guild provided the earliest of all the Trades' chairs, presented by cooper (couper) Jerome Blak in 1574.

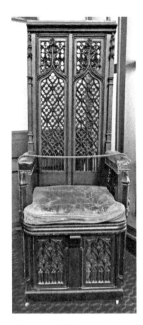

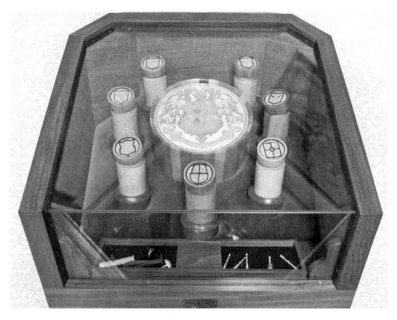

Above left: The earliest Deacon Convener's chair at the Trades Ha' was donated by 'sweird slipper' Matthew Guild, *c.* 1570. Highly ornate, its tracery is believed to be 'tymmer wark of the queyr' removed from St Nicholas Kirk during the Reformation.

Above right: A cooper's essay of eight barrels, each with a carved lid representing all seven Incorporated Trades. Each barrel contains miniature tools belonging to that trade. The seven fit into the larger barrel made by Alan Steele.

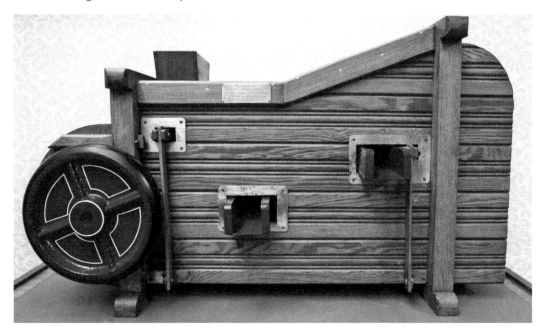

Essay piece of a thrashing mill made by ex-Deacon George Davidson.

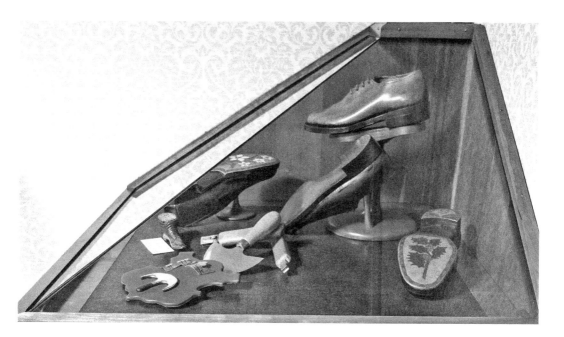

Above: Shoemakers' Incorporation: William L. Reid's essay piece of a pair of shoes, 1934; Lewis S. Stuart's pin-point-worked soles, *c.* 1945; trade tools given to ex-servicemen post-First World War gifted by Thomas Donaldson.

Right: The Hammermen's arms with royal crown, hammer and tower (armourers and swordmakers worked at castles) surrounded by symbols of Hammermen trades.

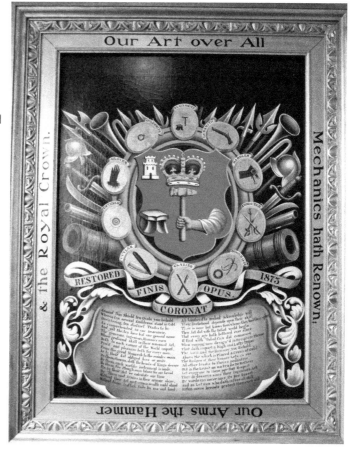

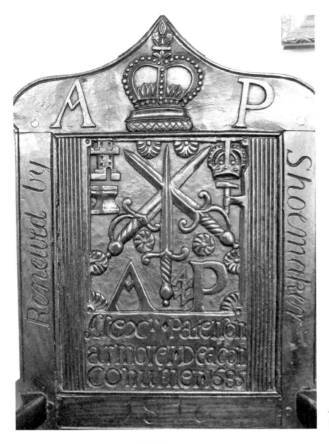

Armourer chair, Deacon Alex Paterson, 1685.

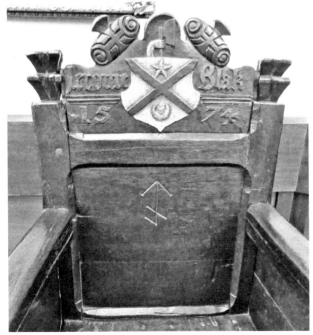

Jerome Blak's family arms of saltire and star signifying military service, with a crescent moon symbolising enlightenment. Projecting from the shield is an arm and hand grasping a coopers' side axe and painted barrels, 1574.

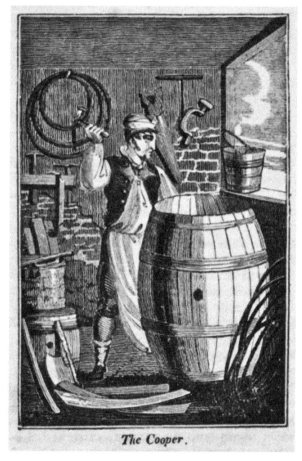

The Cooper.

Cooper.

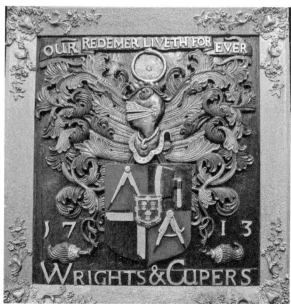

Carved low-relief panel represents
the Wrights and Coopers guild.

The Tailors' crest includes the figure of Eve alongside Adam. While women were able to work at various trades Scotland's male tailors combined to exclude them from all aspects of tailoring. It was Aberdeen's progressive tailors who ended this unfair practice during the 18th century when women were permitted to make clothing for females but still could not be guild members.

Aberdeen's tailors and weavers were radicals and coopers conservative. Towards the end of 1785 as America fought for independence from Britain, tailors and weavers led the domestic struggle for greater openness and fairness in local government. Aberdeen's streets filled with protestors demanding impartiality from the town council whose burgesses were seen to favour some trades over others.

Civic disagreements sometimes became physical. On one memorable occasion a fight broke out on Shiprow between fifty pro-fairness wrights and a group of coopers. The melee continued up Marischal Street and into the Castlegate with the militia giving chase. Three wrights were arrested and locked in the Tolbooth, which in turn was stoned until the prisoners were released. Tension in the town ran high with the Provost and his home both threatened and councillors going into hiding. A trial followed, with defendants either being acquitted or given small fines.

Tailors, incorporated in 1532, were often represented by expanded scissors, bodkins and goose or smoothing irons, but the fascinating Cockie's chair, which folds into a twelve-sided table, displays no trade symbols only Alexander Cockie's family arms – a cock, naturally, the sun and crescent moon between two stars or mullets.

Shoemakers or cordwainers and cordiners were a recognised trade with privileges and obligations in the 1420s. From the start they appear to have had a predilection for keeping voluminous notes and making lengthy statutes governing members, not that this was any guarantee of consistently high standards of work as the town council made clear in 1495 when the trade was criticised for the 'evil werk maid'. This row led to the creation of a Deacon of the craft, responsible for probity and good workmanship.

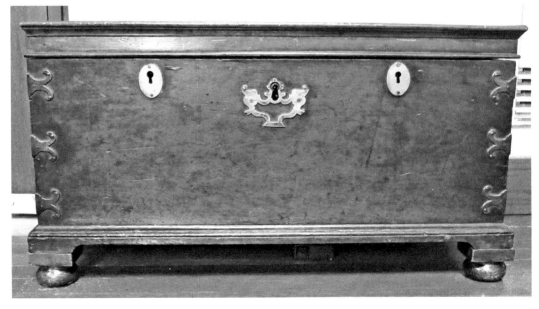

Each trade owned its own kist for preserving documents and money. Three separate key-keepers kept everyone honest.

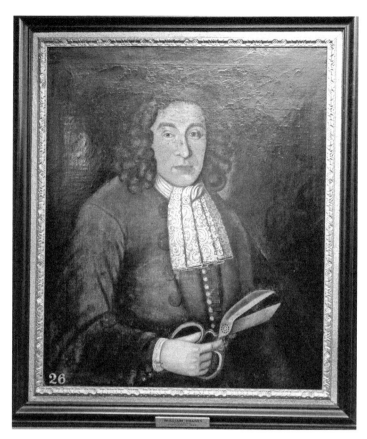

Portrait of William
Phanes, Deacon of the
Tailor Incorporation
of Aberdeen, 1693.
(Artist unknown)

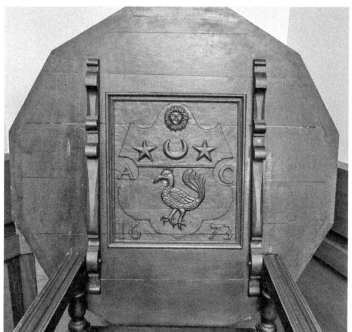

Cockie's chair-cum-
table was presented
by Alexander Cockie,
'taylyer', in 1673.

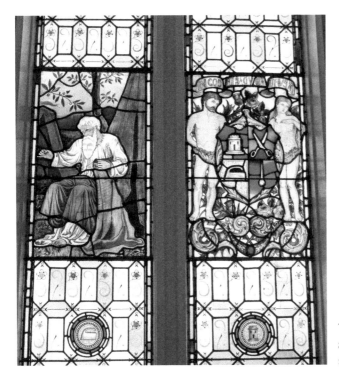

Tailors represented by St Paul as a tent maker in this stained-glass window.

As with quality, so with prices. The town council regulated what a cordiner might charge, whether it was for women's or men's 'dowbill solit schone' (not for poorer Aberdonians). These could be sold at the Schone (shoe) Market with the Deacon Convener keeping a watchful eye for malpractice as he did in 1619 when all shoes failing his test for quality were donated to the city's poor: '…and sic as sall be found spilt, rottin, and insufficient, and yet be of hors ledder sall presentlie be confiscate dealt to ye poore.'

Just as shoemaking was controlled, so too was the processing of hides and leather used for footwear; currier-tanners formed part of the guild. There was scrutiny, too, to prevent illegally imported hides. To this end in 1605 the trade assumed management of the town's Barkmill where hides were taken for curing (tanning) to produce leather. In 1679 Jon Cowper and Andro Galloway were accused of illegally importing 'roch hydes' and bark for tanning, which had not been offered to the cordiners, resulting in higher prices charged to shoemakers. Incorporated shoemakers pleading they were in danger of falling into poverty were saved when the council ruled hides and bark must be sold to cordiners at the lower first price. Shoemakers' influence extended to the slaughter of beasts at butchers' markets much to the displeasure of the fleshers. This was to guard against hides being spoiled by 'cutting, scoreing, or gashing'. They also policed imports of shoes from outside the city, a regulation that James Leslie contravened in the late seventeenth century when he was found guilty of bringing Edinburgh-made shoes to Aberdeen.

Journeymen employed by members of the Shoemakers could be inducted into the trade, but the system faltered for unincorporated men posed a competitive threat. By the eighteenth century this restrictive practice was relaxed to accommodate local 'cobblers' – acknowledging their right to work and trade and in return the 'unfree' men were obliged to contribute towards the Shoemakers' guild.

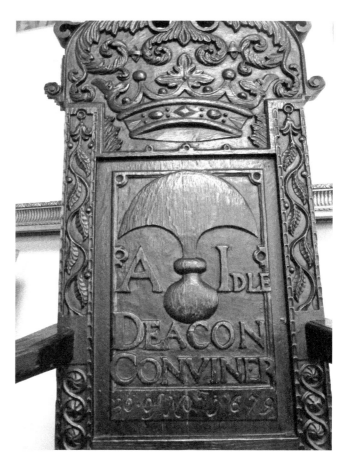

Chair detail: Shoemaker Deacon Convener Alexander Idle, 1679, with ducal crown and cutting knife.

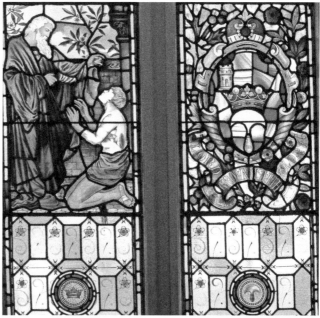

Shoemakers' guild's stained-glass window has the Prodigal Son receiving shoes from his father.

Aberdeen's self-regulation faced more opposition with the arrival of businessmen with small capital intent on opening shops. One such was John Courage from London who in 1758 set up business 'at the sign of the Boot and Shoe' in the Broadgate. Imports of footwear became more common with 'Inglis schone, Frenshe schoon', as the old regulators called them, available to those with the money to buy them.

Recognised by the town council in the fifteenth century, Fleshers were incorporated by 1534. Their contribution to the Seven Incorporated Trades was to provide a lavish annual banquet for members. Fleshers' symbols included knives and hatchets and heads of domesticated animals they slaughtered and sold – rams, sheep, pigs and cattle. Slaughter often took place out in the open, a grisly, bloody practice restricted by the council in 1670 when it forbade slaughter 'upon the streets ... and under the staires ... towards the foire street which was very indecent to be seen'. The previous year the council had been similarly outraged by the open selling of fish on the roadway, contaminated by 'fulzie and filth of the calsie'.

Families of deceased members of trades could hire mort cloths embroidered with their trade symbols. For example, the Fleshers' dark purple cloth carried charges for each use: covering the coffin at the home, covering the coffin between home and church, covering the coffin in church.

Aberdeen's ancient guild of bakers or baxters was formed in 1398 and incorporated in 1532. These craftsmen were once vital members of communities; bread is, after all, the staff of life. At least it once was; now it is probably pizza. At times when few households had ovens, bread dough mixed at home was taken to a bakehouse for baking. Every community had its baker – probably several. There were over sixty bakers and confectioners in Aberdeen's town centre alone in the early 1800s. Any medieval artisan baker wishing to open a shop had to make a maisterstick (mentioned in Aberdeen Bakers' guild regulations of 1579) to be judged by the guild to ascertain his skill and suitability as a master of his craft. Bread was so essential

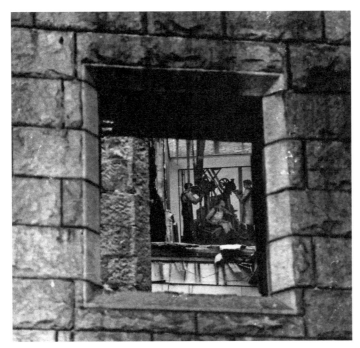

Glimpse of a mural of shoemakers during demolition of the Taranty Ha' on Union Street in 1979.

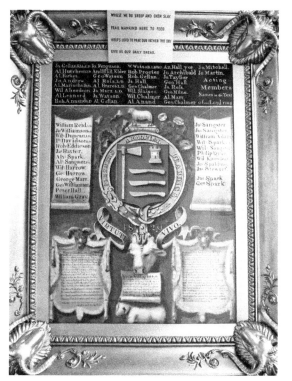

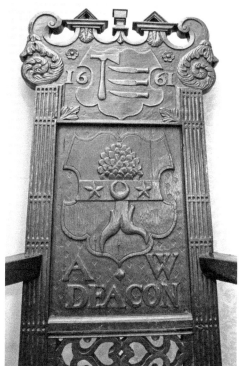

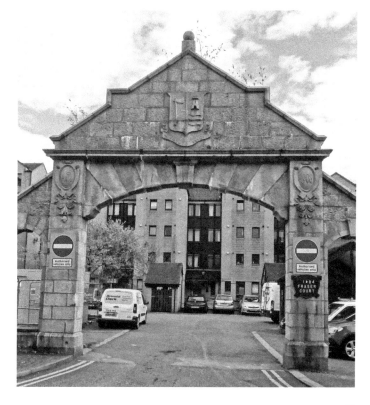

Above left: 'Give us our Daily Bread' in an elaborate representation of the Fleshers' trade. (Painted by 'J. Laing, pictor'.)

Above right: The chair belonging to Deacon Andrew Watson, 1661, is the only mahogany chair in the collection; all others are oak. Note the blood-red-coloured shield and carving of an oak tree.

Right: Entrance to the former abattoir on Hutcheon Street, known locally as the 'killing hoose'.

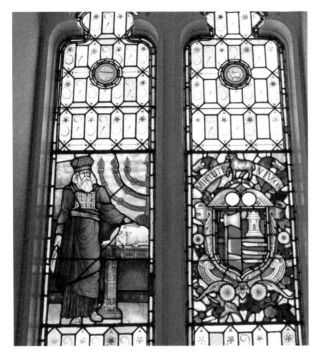

Fleshers' window shows the high priest offering a sacrifice.

to the medieval Scots diet that it was tightly regulated by the town council, which instructed local bakers to make 'penny breid and tua penny breid'.

At the start of the nineteenth century the influence of guilds was on the wane with Aberdeen's craft bakers now organised into a trade union. Before the end of the century, in 1888, at a meeting in the Shiprow Café, a national bakers' organisation was set up. Described as 'a very virile and active body' the Operative Bakers of Scotland National Federal Union was led by Aberdeen bakers; Alexander Catto, who instigated it, was its first chairman. He became the Scottish TUC's first general secretary and was active in establishing the Independent Labour Party.

The Union's main role was to negotiate with employers over pay and working conditions. Bakeries could be dangerous workplaces: burns, trapped limbs, strains, cuts and amputations, splinters and skin irritations all took their toll on employees' health. Bakers worked up to sixteen hours – far in excess of the normal tradesman's day. An attempt to ban night baking in 1848 came to nought, and a century later bakers were still calling for one. Aberdeen Bakers were active in the eight-hour-day movement and advocates for old age pensions.

The old guilds were very protective of their own. Being run by men for men they targeted women trying to earn a living through baking cakes and biscuits at home for sale, forcing them to pay to use bakehouse ovens and restricting the sale of their produce. The guilds successors, trade unions, operated in the same way. Women were tolerated in bakehouses only as cleaners until the First World War when women were encouraged to work in them. Gradually they got a toehold in the trade, beginning with operating pastry mixers for pies and tarts and turning pancakes and oatcakes on hot plates, but they were prevented from handling fermented bread dough. By 1936 bakery women were becoming unionised; they had to be as bakehouses were closed shops. Women's employment was then tightly restricted with quotas based on the number of male employees. Of course women's earning was far lower than their

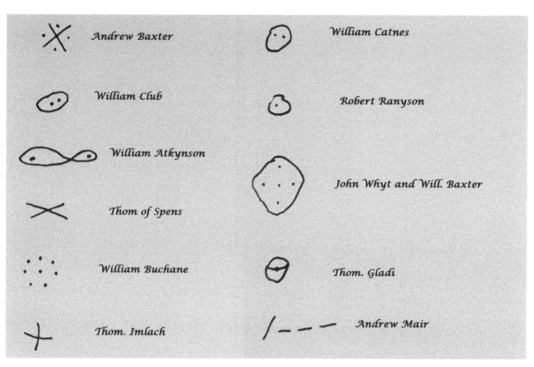

Andrew Baxter

William Catnes

William Club

Robert Ranyson

William Atkynson

John Whyt and Will. Baxter

Thom of Spens

William Buchane

Thom. Gladi

Thom. Imlach

Andrew Mair

In 1458 eleven town bakers were permitted to practise their trade and mark their bread individually.

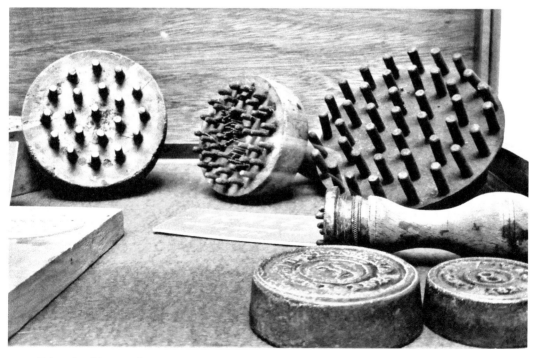

Bakers' tickles used to stamp, *c.* 1800.

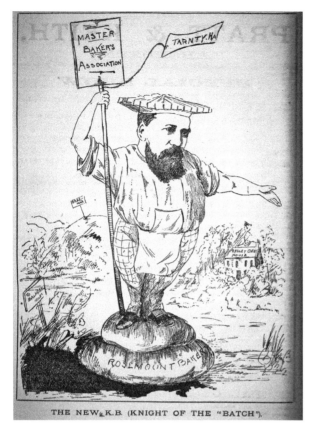

THE NEW K.B. (KNIGHT OF THE "BATCH").

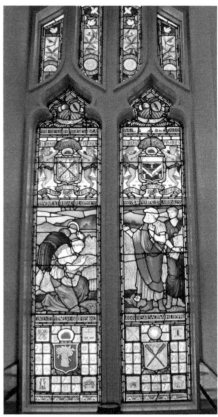

Above left: Delegates to the annual Scottish Bakers' Master Association meeting in June 1892 visited the Persley home of baker John Leadingham.

Above right: Boaz with Ruth gleaning grain and the Bakers' arms and emblems of their trade.

male counterparts; in the 1930s female workers received a maximum of 32s a week – around half that paid to men.

Weavers or wabsters belong to an ancient craft. In Aberdeen they were incorporated in 1449 despite a declaration of the Scots Parliament that the office of deacon was illegal. The incorporated weavers were convicted of acting independently of the town council in 1536. The Weavers' guild included fullers or listers (textile dyers) and waulkers who finessed and prepared cloth. Cloth covered everything from coarse textiles for sails and sacking, blankets and funeral shrouds to finer material for clothing. Aberdeen, in common with many other areas, benefited from skilled migrant weavers from the Low Countries.

The land around Aberdeen provided abundant supplies of sheep wool so it was perhaps inevitable that textiles would become a major source of wealth for local manufacturers and merchants built on the skills of spinners, knitters and weavers; local women, men and children. For the poor the working day was exhausting and extremely long. In 1574 John Cooper was employed to rouse weary workers from their beds at 4 a.m. for the gruelling day ahead:

John Cowpar to pas evrie day in the morning at four houris, and evrie nicht at viii houris [and play upon] quhissil (whistle) ... and on the tabroune, quhairby the craftismen their servandis and all utheris laboriouss folkis being warnit ... may pas to thair labouris and fray their labouris.

When guild privileges were abolished in 1846 restrictions within Trade interactions loosened.

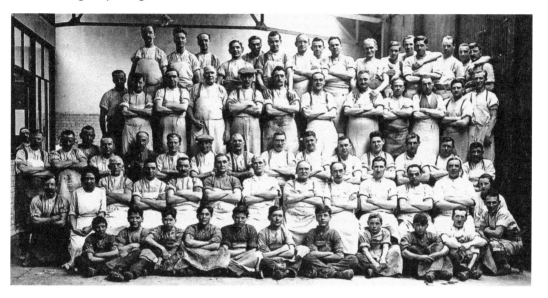

Above: Northern Co-operative bakers at Aberdeen *c.* 1920.

Right: The weavers' motto, 'Spero in Deo et ipse facit ane' (Trust in God and all will be well), their arms of three leopard heads each with a spule or shuttle in their mouths.

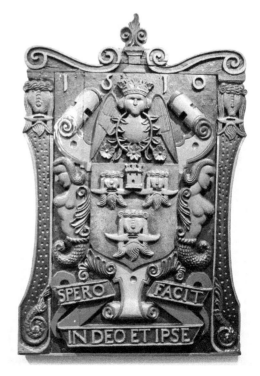

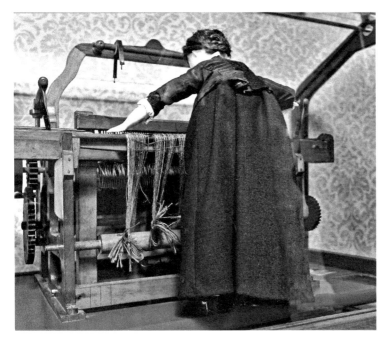

Model of a female handloom weaver from the collection at Aberdeen's Incorporated Trades. As yet women cannot be members of the Incorporated Trades.

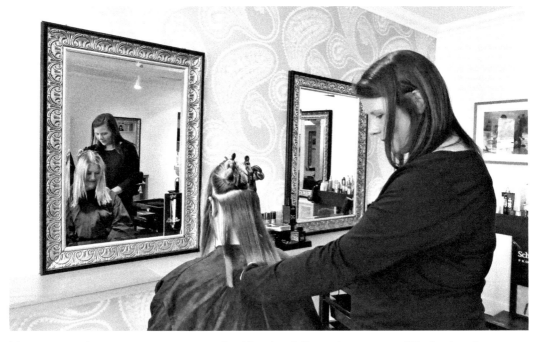

Not every trade or occupation came under Aberdeen's Seven Incorporated Trades. Leechers, barber-surgeons and wig makers had their own trade body. Twenty-first-century stylist Stephanie Douglas dresses colleague Amy Father's hair at Sarah Franklin's salon.

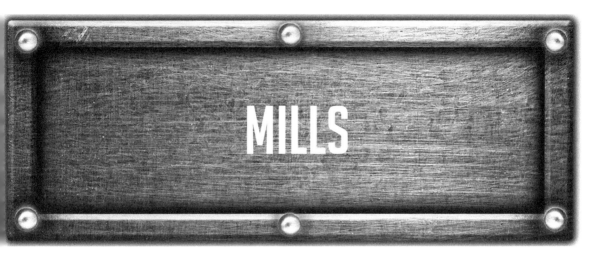

MILLS

I ken some folk look doon on us and ca' us orra trag,
But hearts may love and thochts be pure the' cover'd by a rag;
On Feersday night when wages comes I pay a' that I'm due,
An' wir the auld claes oot until I'm able to get new,
Until I can get new, takin' up nae shooster's bill,
For I'll try to be aye clear o' debt tho' wirkin at the mill.

William Carnie, *A Factory Lassie's Song* (1980)

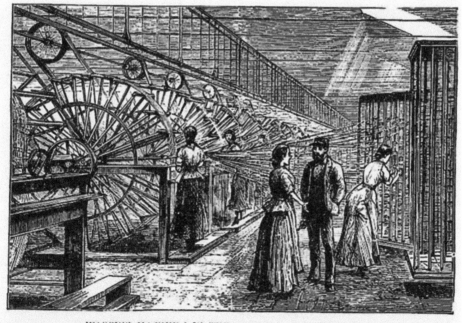

WARPING MACHINES IN THE GRANDHOLM TWEED MILLS

Warping machines, Grandholm, 1880s.

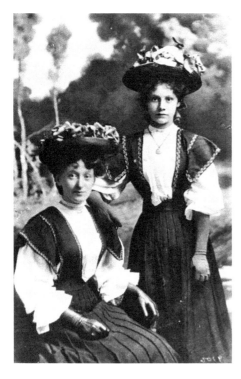

Lizzie Smith, seated, and her half-sister, Jane Brown, both linen weavers at Broadford's, lived in Gilcomston's Stevenson Street. This photograph *c.* 1890/1900 shows them 'on the razzle' on a day off according to Lizzie's grandson Alan Robertson. (Courtesy of Alan Robertson)

Aberdeen had many sorts of manufactories or mills – snuff, waulk, whin, meal, printing, paper, etc. – but textile production was for a long time the most important of all. Cloth from wool, linen and cotton were all produced in Aberdeen. Flax grows readily in Scotland, and the linen it produced became a significant export during the eighteenth and nineteenth centuries. Gordon, Barron & Co.'s manufactory at Woodside employed 3,000 hands spinning cotton thread and weaving. Into the nineteenth century and Forbes, Low & Company was one of four cotton mills in the town, using steam power at its Poynernook mill. This factory was eventually sold to Pirie & Sons for envelope and coloured paper production.

Gordon's Mills on the Don were used by various businesses such as Leys, Still & Co. from 1749 to produce thread and a range of textiles. It was here around 1775 that Gordon and Barron, in partnership with Alexander Milne and Duguid, took out a lease on 23 acres of land for a mill, bleachfield and printfield. English millowner Arkwright was an acquaintance of Milne, who sent his workers to Derbyshire to learn mill skills, which they brought back to Aberdeen.

Mills employed children as well as adults. They were known as bun boys or bound boys and were housed in a large building called the Barracks. The greatest number of millhands were women, with around 2,000 employed during the 1790s – far more than boys and men. Cloth production, however, depended on more than mill labour. Independent handloom weavers were vital suppliers of textiles. Scattered around the north-east, including Arduthie at Stonehaven and Bankhead, they sold cloth to Gordon, Barron & Company.

The roughest linen produced from flax mills on Donside went for ship sails, sacking and Osnaburgs, which sold well in the Netherlands and England. In fact, it was popular in Britain's colonies for slave clothing because of its hard-wearing if rough properties, and it was very cheap. Exported to America, it covered wagons – the large prairie schooners used by immigrants heading west.

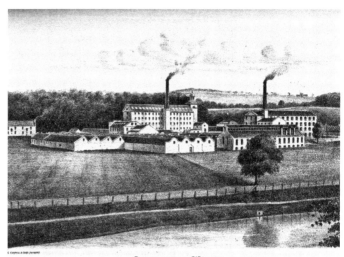

GRANDHOLM WORKS.
Formerly Messrs Leys, Mason & Co now Messrs J & J. Crombie.

Grandholm Mills.

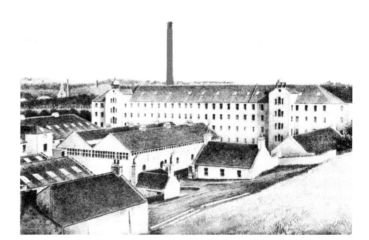

Grandholm Mills.

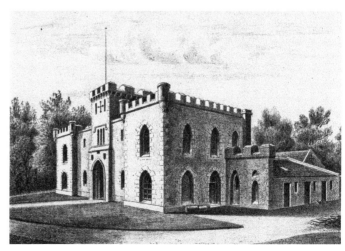

Woodside Barracks
where textile mill children
were housed.

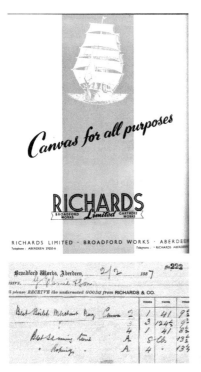

Sail canvas from Richards for schooner *Mercury*, 1887.

Wool from Aberdeenshire's farms was spun for knitting or woven to make plaids and blankets. Large-scale production of woollen cloth began around 1748 at both Donside and Garlogie, west of the town. Millions of pounds of wool were spun annually and woven into woollen cloth, but Aberdeen's distance from large ports meant it was disadvantaged against English mills with easy access to bigger markets. On the other hand wages were lower in Aberdeen than in England and the Don provided plenty fast-running water to drive mill wheels – perhaps not swift enough for some. Management at Leys & Co. hired a gang of men to steal barrows and spades from Aberdeen harbour under cover of darkness, which they used to deepen and widen the Persley Canal to increase flow to the mill.

With steam power dependency on water declined, heralding changes to the physical landscape, the organisation of labour and removing the impact of the vagaries of climate on power. By the 1830s when the city population was 60,000 around 13,000 people around Aberdeen worked in textiles. Both sexes and all ages made the daily trudge to buildings as big as cathedrals, but with none of their spiritual uplift.

Notoriously long working hours that began with the early morning shrill whistle to waken exhausted workers were addressed in 1833 when Factory Commissioners met with Aberdeen's mill owners who insisted shorter hours would damage their industry and only benefit foreign competitors. Some variation existed across the local manufacturers, but a normal week amounted to seventy-two hours composed of six days for mill-hands, including children as young as nine, ever under scrutiny and the whip-hand of an overseer. Most mills would only take children of ten and over, but as Thomas Leys Hadden of Grandholm Mill explained, his mill would employ younger children 'chiefly to oblige poor parents who live in the neighbourhood of the works, and who otherwise cannot support them'. Children were an essential part of the labour force. Patrick Pirie of Gordon's Mills told Commissioners that the

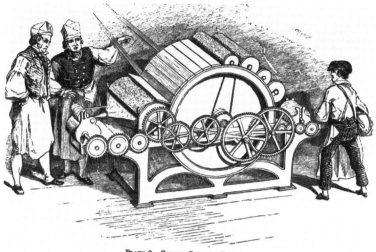

Carding machine of the 1840s, for processing fibre prior to spinning.

PLATE 2.—COTTON CARDING ENGINE.

very machinery at his manufactory was designed to accommodate workers of small stature, 'not intended to be worked by full-grown persons'. Of course mills were dangerous work places and there were frequent and horrific accidents, such as in 1821 when a child died after falling into boiling liquid.

Hadden's mill, in the Green, dominated Aberdeen city centre. This vast enterprise had grown from small beginnings when young Alexander Hadden borrowed £5 to buy hand-knitted stockings, which he sold on at markets at the likes of Stonehaven and Banchory. The stockings knitted by countrywomen – 'shank wives' – around Aberdeen formed the basis of Scotland's hosiery trade, which was enormously popular with customers in Holland and Germany and mushroomed into an immense business. Back in 1695 stockings were exported by the Company of Scotland to Africa and the Indies as part of Scotland's attempt to benefit from opportunities offered by these emerging markets. In the end Scotland's international trade was diminished through the imposition of England's Navigation Acts and subsequent attacks on Scottish merchant ships on the high seas. This aggressive behaviour only ceased with the Union of Scotland with England when Scottish commerce was absorbed into British trade.

At just eight years old Thomas Edwards was already working at Grandholm Mills. This was in 1822 when children like him worked the same wearing hours as adults: yokin was 6 a.m. and lousin at 8 p.m. Living some 2 miles from his work, Thomas Edwards rose at 4 a.m. and returned home at 9 p.m.

During his two years at Grandholm Thomas was trained in heckling, carding and spinning and received anything from 3 to 4 shillings a week. As horrified as we might be by this working regime, Thomas Edward 'liked this factory. It was a happy time for me'. The contentment he found was born of the rural setting: 'It teemed with nature and natural objects. The woods were easy of access during our meal hours.' Monday to Friday workers were given two forty-five-minute meal breaks daily, but the shorter Saturday hours, ending at 5 p.m. meant they had only one break, making the total working week around seventy hours. Sam Howarth was nine in 1812 when he began work. As an old man he spoke of over eighty years service at the mill and the good feelings he had towards his time there, adding its owners treated him well, 'were very kind … give me a pension so I am very well'.

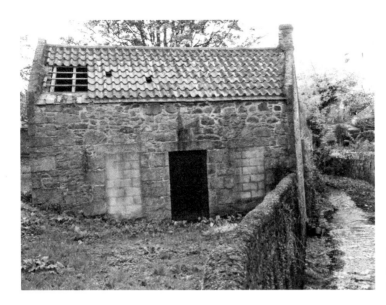

Remains of a weaver's
workshop by
the Denburn.

By and large millworkers were unskilled and lacked capital so were dependent on factory employment; as long as business was buoyant their jobs were secure. However, mass production gave work on the one hand and destroyed livelihoods on the other. Like in so many Scottish towns Aberdeen's community of handloom weavers, notably in the Gilcomston area, were skilled men and women, celebrated both for the quality of their cloth and their independent spirit. Weaving was a family undertaking, as Alexander Bain who was born in Skene Square in 1818 recorded: 'rocking the cradle of a baby, fetching water (a standing need), or assisting in the home part of a weaver's work – namely filling the little bobbins with yarn for the shuttles – a duty that fell primarily to the weaver's wife, but which was ultimately shared in by the children.'

Hard-worked mill children received a wage – however paltry. The children of handloom weavers did not; bed, board, education and affection was their reward, always dependent in the last instance on the weaver's demeanour and luck in negotiating a price for cloth. Within the weaver's shop hours were also long and challenging for young children, only an arm's length away from a skelp from a frustrated parent who dictated the rhythm and rate of activity in contrast to the mill with its machinery revolving to the pace set by water or steam. Mills, however, were inherently more dangerous workplaces with revolving belts, rotating gears and flying shuttles.

Poynernook resident William Cadenhead spent a lifetime in Aberdeen's textile industries, starting as a ten year old in a thread factory in Carmelite Street. This was around the tail end of the handloom weavers' dominance, when they still commanded respect and often good prices for their cloth – what Aberdeen weaver poet William Thom described as the 'daisy portion of weaving'. Cadenhead wrote:

> O, happy weavers once did thrive
> Whase fair day's work did mair than earn
> A scanty meal for wife and bairns
> And left a cluschach I' the moggan
> In times of stress to keep them joggin.

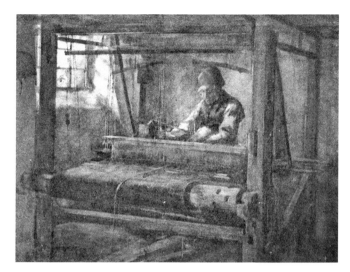

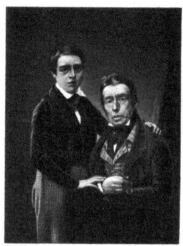

Above left: Weaver's shop from an illustration by Henry W. Kerr.

Above right: Weaver-poet William Thom and son.

It is a moot point how much of any good 'daisy' days earnings weavers shared with their families. Handloom weavers apparently liked to 'hae a guid claik' (gossip) with fellow craftsmen. Many were political radicals and were partial to liquor, as was Thom, but other weavers supported temperance and total abstinence. Weaver-botanist John Duncan belonged to this latter group. Originally from Stonehive, south of Aberdeen, he began working at Leys, Masson & Company in 1818 as a handloom weaver in a large workshop alongside others also dependent on this single firm for their income, and subject to the discipline of an overseer. Independent-minded Duncan rejected these constraints and chose life as an itinerant 'country weaver', seeking work in the small weavers' shops that serviced local communities across Aberdeenshire. Webs woven by these rural weavers were to order and the finished cloth passed to a local tailor – also semi-itinerant and travelling from village to village and house to house, staying a day or two to complete articles of clothing. Tailors' earnings were agreed as a daily fee plus board and lodging – a method of tailoring known as 'whipping the cat'. Duncan's lifestyle gave him a poor living, but allowed him a certain amount of liberty denied factory handloom weavers to pursue other interests – in his case collecting and studying the area's flora.

Handloom weavers increasingly lost their relative economic autonomy as the dominance of a few textile merchants grew with commercial power becoming concentrated in fewer hands. In his autobiography Alexander Bain noted:

> It was the sad experience of our family that the remuneration of piece work steadily fell from year to year; and my earliest feelings of bitter distress were due to my father's announcing time after time the reduction of the rate per piece of the fabrics that he wove … for a number of years his working day ranged from thirteen to fifteen hours.

The profitable rush of powerlooms sounded the end for traditional handloom weavers. William Cadenhead captured their despair when he wrote that labour 'feels each new

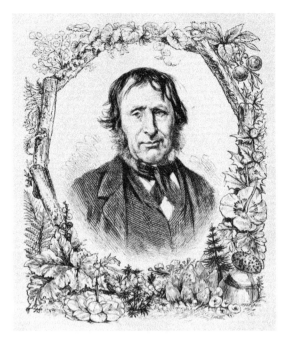

John Duncan, weaver and botanist.

invention as the signal for fresh slaughter'. They were victims of the inexorable march of factory production and erosion of older traditional crafts. Yet some weavers saw positives in the system. Weaver George Smith was familiar with mill life and described the millhands as 'slave o' slaves'; nonetheless, he believed the vast power that was harnessed to expand industry provided the world with greater material benefits, even if these tended to fall into the hands of 'laird or lord'.

In Smith's poem 'The Twa Waters, Dee and Don' the largely unexploited River Dee expresses ironic sympathy for its northern counterpart, the Don, as a waterway constrained by dykes in order to drive mills 'tormented driving wheels … and rising ilka morning by the bell'. The Don scornfully responds boasting of its ability to take the,

> …flaxen stores of Russia … silks o' India … to me
> Old Smyrna sends her cotton store … English wool
> is spun by me … The vera sarks your greatest lairds
> put on received their whiteness frae the streams o' Don.

Aberdeen's first mills were water-powered, with many along the banks of the Don at lands of Cruives, Woodside. Donside's geology, the result of glacial movements, had created steep gradients so that the Don ran faster downhill to the sea at Aberdeen than the quiet flowing Dee and was more useful for turning waterwheels. Thus it was the Don that came to be exploited for its ability to drive mills, which provided employment for generations of Aberdonians. People came to depend on them for work like later generations of Aberdonians would depend on the oil and gas industries in the twentieth and twenty-first centuries. Both sectors provided livings for thousands when markets were buoyant but were incapable of holding off outside pressures, resulting in fluctuating levels of employment. Grandholm Mills finally closed its doors in 1991 with production, including the famous Crombie brand moving south, followed thirteen years later by the contraction of Richards Broadford works, transferring to Granitehill and thereafter liquidation with workers left, as they say, on the scrapheap and fighting for their pensions. With the closure of Richards' main works the city centre link with textiles was severed and with it that bond to the early Industrial Revolution.

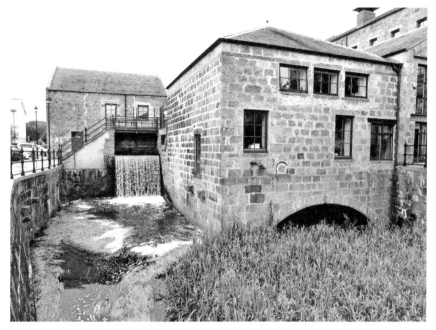

Grandholm, lade sluice gates and water turbine house, 2019.

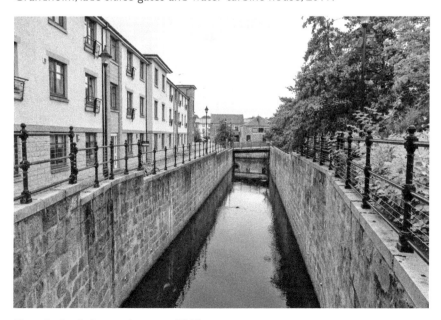

Grandholm, lade running east, 2019.

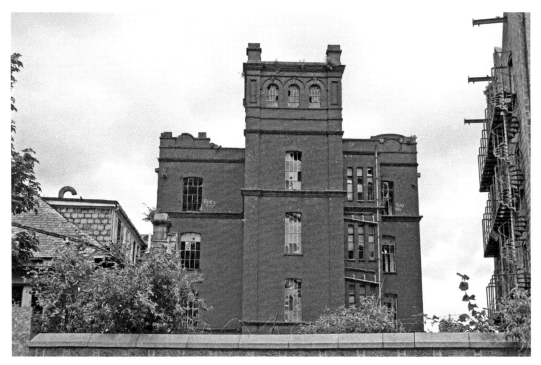

Richards Broadford mill stands abandoned. Startling red brick and grey granite Aberdeen, 2018.

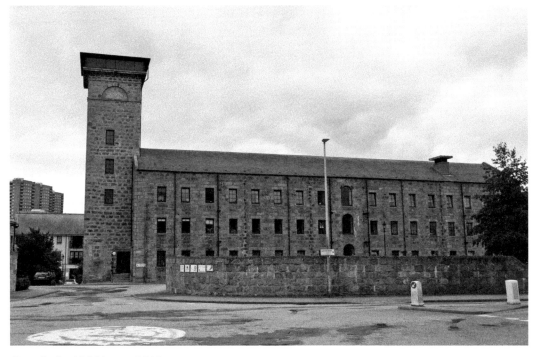

Grandholm Mill House, 2019.

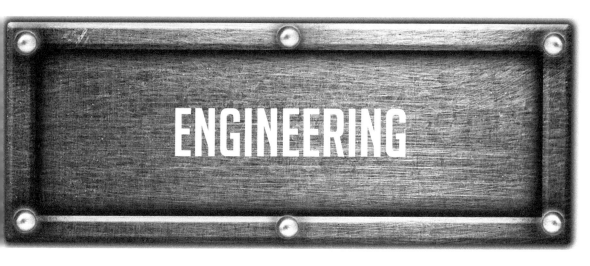

ENGINEERING

Metal-working industries were truly a nineteenth-century phenomena, providing work for thousands. Skills nurtured in small workshops of wrights and blacksmiths were transferred to larger enterprises using ever-more powerful and complex machinery while other manufacturing processes such as shoemaking relied largely on handicraft skills, which would be easily recognisable to medieval tradesmen.

Aberdeen's metal industries, including shipbuilding, never grew to the extent they did farther south because of the city's need to import coal and iron from far afield, its distance from markets and Aberdeen's relatively small population. Nonetheless, her businessmen and workforces had an impact on the vast market of nineteenth-century industrial capital.

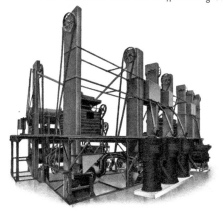

"BON-ACCORD" Plantation Machinery

RENOWNED wherever Rice and Coffee are grown

SELF-CONTAINED RICE MILL

Manufactured by

WM. McKINNON & CO. LTD.
SPRING GARDEN IRON WORKS · ABERDEEN

Cable and Telegraphic Address : "AMPANG ABERDEEN"

ESTABLISHED 1798—OVER 150 YEARS OF SERVICE

William Mckinnon, Rice Mill, c. 1950.

William McKinnon's company provides an example of how expanding colonial markets created fresh opportunities for trade. For the first sixty years following its founding in 1798 McKinnon's millwrights made and supplied equipment and sold guano and crushed bones for fertilisers locally. By the 1860s McKinnon's was supplying plantation machinery for processing coffee, cacao and rice – commodities at the heart of British exploitation of the colonies, with Britain regarded as the 'home' country, acquiring raw materials and processing them into highly profitable industrial commodities. John Gordon from Deeside promoted such trade. Having spent seven years in Ceylon he returned to London in the 1850s and set up his Colonial Engineers business. Gordon's familiarity with the colonies meant he was an ideal negotiator for British companies, such as McKinnon's, seeking imperial contracts. With changing times the company declined and its city-centre premises with only twenty-eight remaining workers was closed in 1993; the workshops and iron foundry were demolished. With the closure of McKinnon's the city probably lost its last iron foundry, breaking the town's link to the Industrial Revolution.

Traditional mechanical engineers John M. Henderson and Barry, Henry & Cook are also long gone from the city. Presented with the opportunity to win government development grants in 1985, Henderson's moved from its Kings Works to Arbroath. The company was founded by Aberdonian John Henderson, who, having served his time with local firm Abernethy, left the city to broaden his experience. He returned in the 1860s and eventually formed a brief partnership with James Adam at a workshop in Jopp's Lane, described as 'vomiting out dense volumes of smoke'. The firm first depended on work from local farmers such as modifying horse-driven thrashing mills to operate with steam power.

The Henderson & Adam partnership ended in the 1870s, by which time John Henderson's aspirations had grown. He transferred his business to premises on King Street and established an international reputation for the quality and efficiency of its mechanical handling equipment, especially cranes and cableways. Aberdeen's granite trade looked to Henderson to design, manufacture and erect equipment for handling heavy stone in yards and quarries. Henderson

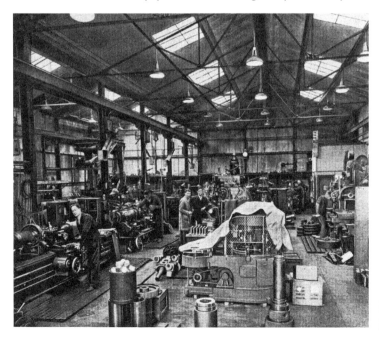

Machine shop
J. M. Henderson, 1940s.

worked for granite master Alexander Macdonald in the 1860s when this stone trade innovator was experimenting with new methods of cutting and polishing granite.

Still a presence in Aberdeen when oil arrived in the city, Henderson's, nevertheless, continued to concentrate on manufacturing machinery for the steel industry rather than the 'black gold' sector. The decision to specialise in equipment for the steel industry was taken when steel was still of some importance to Britain's economy. By this time Aberdeen's granite trade was largely moribund and heavy-lifting mobile cranes were starting to replace Henderson's iconic fixed derrick cranes.

Next door to Henderson's on King Street were engineers Barry, Henry & Co. (later Barry, Henry & Cook), their names immortalised on many cast-iron gulley covers and branders across Aberdeen. The firm's origins can be traced back to the 1790s when they manufactured iron castings and bone manure. All this changed in 1890 when farmer Charles Cook bought the business hoping to boost his son Charles' career. Immediately he poached four engineers from John Harper's engineering company, which was then in Albion Street but was about to move to Balnagask. Such was the ill feeling created between the two businesses Harper sued Barry, Henry & Co. for breach of copyright, alleging Harper's catalogue of castings and power transmission equipment had been plagiarised. With many years' experience in mechanical engineering between them, the four engineers must have been hugely beneficial to Barry, Henry & Co. The company went on to manufacture conveyors, gearing and a wide range of millwright products, including waterwheels – said to be a 'pretty good country trade' with colonial as well as local customers. Charles Cook invested enough capital to make the company one of Aberdeen's chosen munitions factories in the First World War.

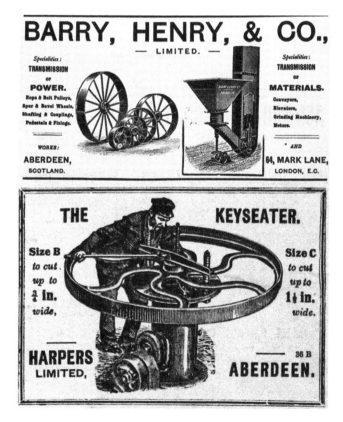

Barry, Henry & Co. and Harpers adverts, 1907 and 1909.

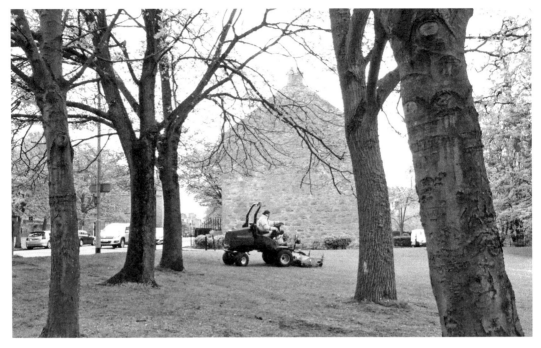

Grass cutter at Gilcomston.

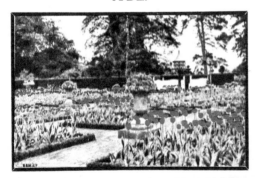
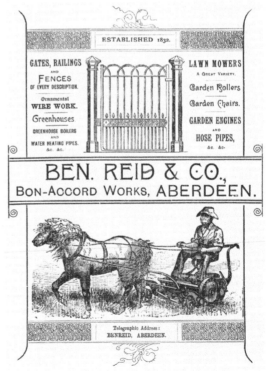
Ben Reid & Co., seedsman, adverts, 1894 and 1932.

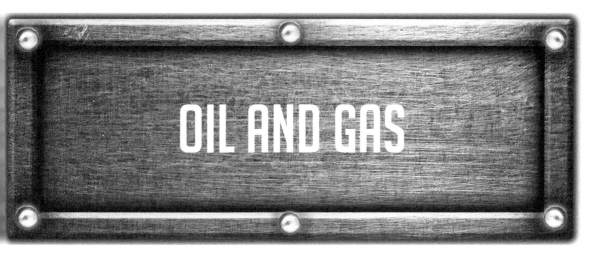

OIL AND GAS

When large oil deposits were discovered in the North Sea off the coast of north-east Scotland Aberdeen found itself transformed from 'Granite City' to 'Oil Capital of Europe'. Suddenly there were jobs galore, with buses, cars, trains and planes packed full of people seeking work – skilled and unskilled. At the skilled end Aberdeen was transformed into a world leader of innovative technology and offshore-related engineering. Thousands of jobs in a host of allied occupations emerged at the start of oil in the 1970s, many based on engineering with time-served men able to take advantage of the arrival of petroleum to start up their own businesses – and for a number this Klondike transformed

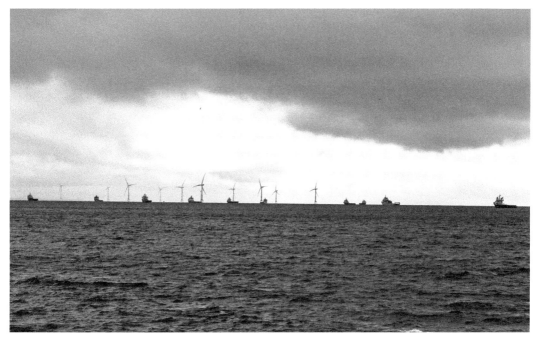

Oil support vessels lying off Aberdeen harbour, alongside the 'competition' – green energy offshore wind farm, 2019.

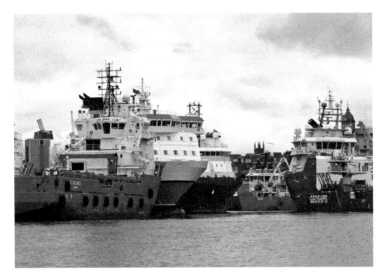

Aberdeen harbour with oil supply vessels, 2012.

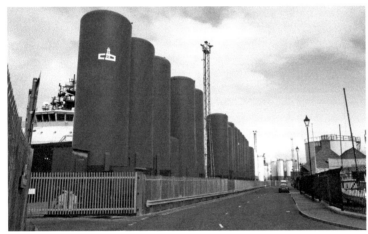

Ubiquitous in 'Oil Capital' Aberdeen, storage tanks characterise the industry almost as much as supply and support vessels, Fittie 2019.

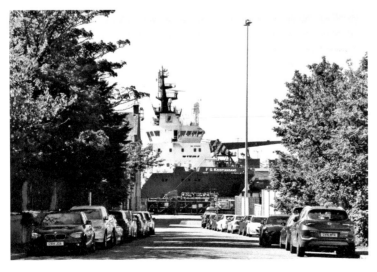

Offshore tug-supply vessel *F S Kristiansand* berthed at the foot of Church Street, Fittie, 2019.

them from wage earners to millionaires. During the early years of North Sea oil and gas even unskilled workers offshore earned high wages, around double the UK average, in exchange for long working hours. Aberdeen bucked the UK trend with very low levels of unemployment. International and small local companies operated on a tide of wealth for all servicing the subsea sector.

One local firm that started in a small way when North Sea oil and gas was in its infancy is Whittaker Engineering at Stonehaven, south of Aberdeen. Ken Whittaker set up his multimillion-pound global business in 1983 from a caravan and shed. Typical of successful companies, Whittaker's adapted to the ever-changing demands of the oil and gas industry through investment in the latest technology and skilled workforce.

In 2019 around ninety Whittaker's employees worked onshore with others offshore, and the company has a subsidiary business in Mexico. Whittaker's success is partly due to the proficiency of its engineers and tradesmen, plus its commitment to producing a workforce for the future. It is a major promoter of apprenticeships, always having twenty-two training at any one time. As each apprentice finishes his or her time, another is recruited to maintain the number. Apprentices are taught all aspects of Whittaker's work, covering different skills such as fabrication, welding, pipefitting, mechanical, de-commissioning, machining and design. While the technology used at Whittaker's is state of the art, apprentice engineers can begin their training on manual machines to help them understand the skills and techniques that underpin the industry. A large percentage of Whittaker's apprentices remain with the company following the completion of their apprenticeships and several employees have spent their entire working lives there.

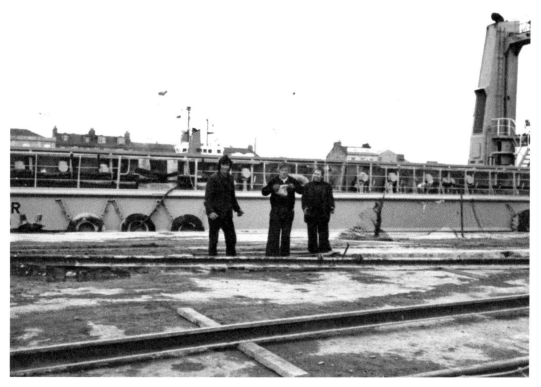

At work beside supply vessel, 1980s.

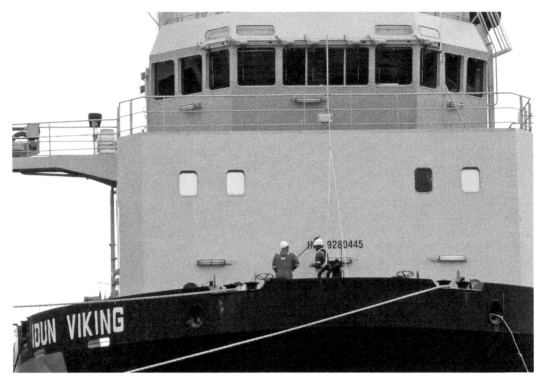

Idun Viking, offshore supply vessel in Aberdeen harbour, 2012. Built in 2003 by Karmsund of Norway, this vessel typified naval architecture associated with servicing the oil industry – far removed from fishing boats, which once were the staple of the working port.

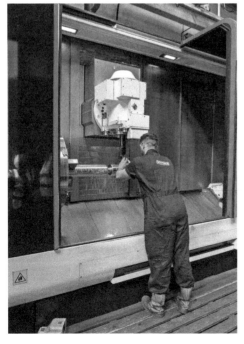

A modern lathe. Fully integrated for turning and milling, digitally programmed by the 'machinist', the machine, fully enclosed during the operation, carries out the instruction. New skills, generally quieter, cleaner and safer than old manual machines. (Whittaker Engineering 2019)

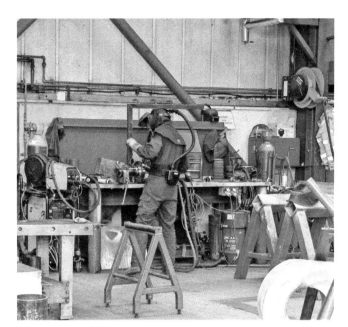

The modern welder not only with eye protection is also suited-up with respiratory headgear. (Whittaker Engineering 2019)

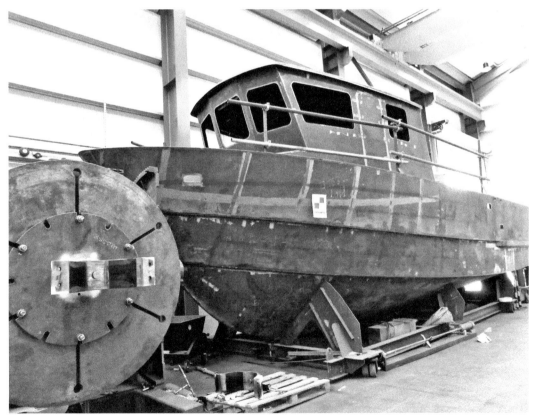

Boat built by welding apprentices during the 2015/2016 oil downturn using their engineering skills. (Whittaker Engineering)

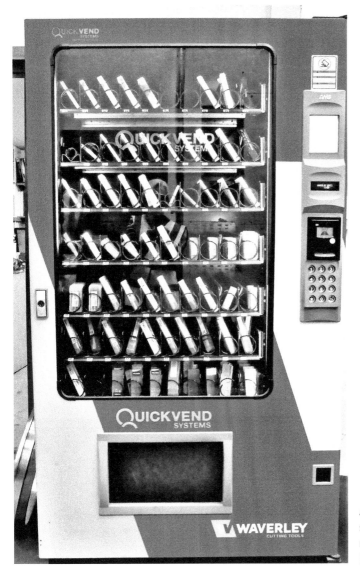

A modern 'tool store' as a vending machine. (Whittaker Engineering 2019)

All component production is computer programmed and much machining is carried out in enclosed compartments, making present-day engineering very much safer than in the past. Now engineers set the programme, set tools for each job and wait for its completion – similar to setting a washing machine's wash programme. What is different from washing machines is that some of this high-tech equipment can cost upwards of £1 million and sometimes double that amount; for example, the company owns an equivalent of a 3-D printer, which can, using a welding technique, turn out steel components of virtually any size by building in layers. It is envisaged in the near future that large structures could be constructed this way. The sheer variety of work offered at Whittaker through its multi-skilled tradesmen means the company can carry out all aspects of design, fabrication and machine processes in-house, with final certification carried out by independent third parties.

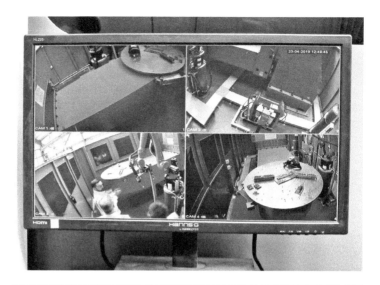

In future 3-D robotic welding such as this will potentially manufacture ships/bridges/steel forgings and more. Using similar technology, a German-Japanese company produces aeroplane wings. (Whittaker Engineering 2019)

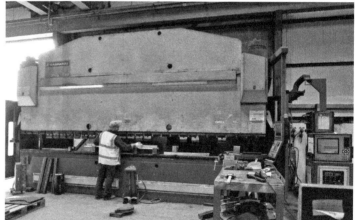

Gasparini RSG 330 Press Brake machine at Whittaker Engineering, 2019.

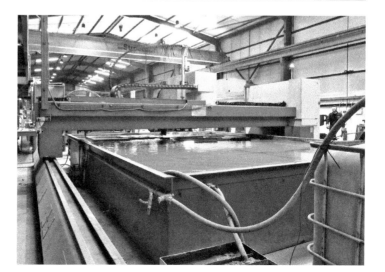

Water jet-cutting machine uses high pressure to accurately slice through any material. It can profile shapes, and create holes and slots where required. Before water jet-cutters this process would have been flame-cut. (Whittaker Engineering, 2019)

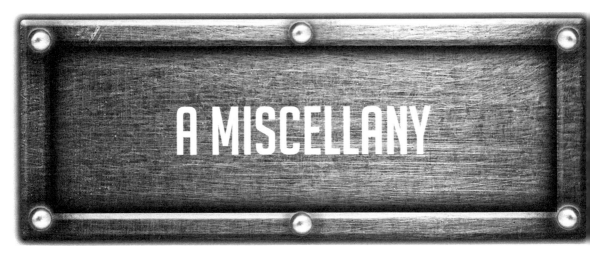

A MISCELLANY

BREWING AND DISTILLING

The happenstance of rich agricultural lands to the west, a bustling harbour on the German Ocean and railways meant Aberdeen's brewers and distillers could produce drink for more than the local market.

As synonymous as whisky is with drinking in Scotland, it was ale and beer many turned to quench their thirst and to enjoy the convivial atmosphere of inn or tavern. Pure drinking water was not always readily available until relatively recent times, and tea and coffee were priced beyond the pocket of many.

Gilcomston and Devanha are probably the two best known Aberdeen breweries, producing ales, beer, stout and porter. Gilcomston brewery occupied a site owned by the town council and adjacent to a town mill immediately north-west of the Castlegate. William Black, renowned Gilcomston brewer, also operated the mill from which he sold barley and peasemeal. Competitors in the early nineteenth century were local, with many small-time enterprises scattered about the town including at Barkmill, the Hardgate, Holburn Street, Virginia Street, Gilcomston Steps and one George Sim at North Street. Some of these establishments might now be described as microbreweries – taprooms that produced their own beers as happened at the Queen Street tavern, a coaching inn later renamed the Banks of Ythan Inn.

In 1807 William Black sold his lease on Gilcomston to concentrate on the Devanha brewery, which had easier access to the harbour. Given suitable tides vessels could sail up the Dee as far as Craiglug to discharge cargoes of grain and ship out drink for export. Black's new enterprise became an opportunity to celebrate, and in 1808 he played host to a 'large party of fashionables' guests including Sir Alexander Bannerman, the Duchess of Gordon and Lord Huntly, who 'drank the health of their host in his delicious brown stout'. Not to be left out, brewery workers 'were enabled liberally to regale themselves after the work of the day'. Fearful that unscrupulous publicans would pass off an inferior product as Devanha's, the brewery issued signage to legitimate publicans bearing the slogan 'Black Entre'.

Gilcomston Brewery's production survived a hiccup in the 1820s over a tussle concerning rights to draw water from the town's supply. In 1843 Gilcomston was put up for sale during a period of business uncertainty, and the brewery was still on the market twelve months later. With deep pockets and business optimism the Bakers of the Incorporated Trades took over the grain mill and brewery and challenged the town's water charge, arguing

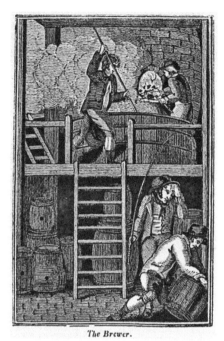

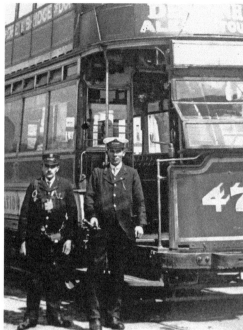

The Brewer.

Above left: Brewer.

Above right: Devanha Brewery advert on Bridges tram number 47.

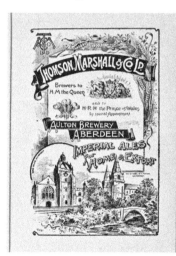

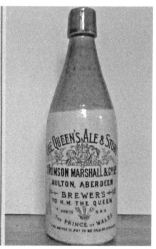

For over a century Aulton Brewery quenched the thirsts of drouthy Aberdonians. Originally trading as Old Aberdeen Brewery, its final days were under the management of Thomson, Marshall & Co., who in a linguistic irony went into liquidation in 1901.

the business was a 'charitable institution' since profits went into a fund supporting guild members. The council remained defiant and won this battle. Eventually the Bakers sold out to Devanha Brewery and so ended a long tradition of brewing at Gilcomston. Devanha itself was put up for sale in 1909 and while it continued to trade under its old name brewing gradually ceased, with only bottling remaining until finally the premises became a warehouse for Usher's and Alloa ales. With changing times Aberdeen cast aside restrictions more suited to medieval commerce than nineteenth-century free markets. For brewers this affected the legacy of the town's responsibilities and rights over the milling of grain. Smaller brewers complained of high costs and inferior grain provided from that pestilent 'dam and filthy burn' at Justice Mills, and in the 1870s they petitioned the council to abolish the obligation, known as multures, to use town mills. The council refused, but the petition highlighted this commercial anachronism, especially in light of a proposal for a privately owned mill to be built in Cotton Street.

As for usquebaugh, the water of life, Aberdeen's population attracted whisky producers from all around the area – legal or not (mainly not). Isolated spots in the countryside relatively close to the town provided perfect cover for setting up illicit stills to make whisky that was smuggled into the town on the backs of men and ponies under cover of darkness.

William Smith was a devout man, but one who enjoyed a tipple. He set up his distillery in 1822 at Jericho, a few miles from Aberdeen, using water from the Jordan burn. Bere barley and wild airborne yeasts went into the making of his Jericho whisky, later renamed Benachie, by which time it was legal. Once legitimate it was openly transported by horse and cart to Insch railway station and on to Aberdeen for sale. The distillery closed early in the twentieth century, a consequence of heavy government duties on Scotland's national drink that priced it beyond the pockets of many.

PAPER MILLS

Paper production began in Aberdeen at the end of the 1600s under Patrick Sandilands of Cotton at Gordon's Mills. Following on from him James Moir set up his paper mill at Stoneywood.

As European migrant craftsmen had influenced textile production in Aberdeen so too did they with the town's paper making, with involvement of French papermakers Nicolas de Champ and Nicolas Dupin. Paper was made from rag cloth until the late nineteenth century when wood pulp was introduced. All types of paper were manufactured in Aberdeen: newspaper, fancy, brown, card, envelopes, writing paper and bags.

The fast-flowing River Don powered papermills at Donside, Stoneywood, Mugiemoss and Inverurie while Culter Mill was set up in Deeside. Davidson's Mugiemoss mill opened in 1796 and closed 2005. The Davidsons were farmers at Tarland before Iyster John Davidson moved his family to Bucksburn north of the town. His son Charles then became a millwright at Grandholm waulkmill until 1811 when he set up his own mill at Mugiemoss to waulk (washing and beating) cloth, beat flax and grind fermented tobacco leaf for snuff. A decade on and he

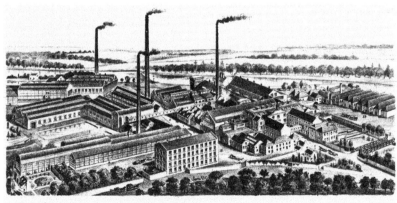

STONEYWOOD PAPER WORKS.
Messrs A.Pirie & Sons. Ltd

Stoneywood.

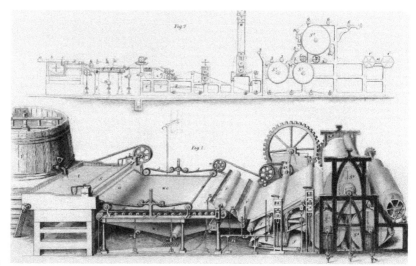

Papermaking machine, 1850s.

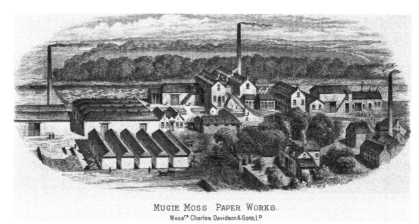

Davidson's Mugiemoss works.

MUGIE MOSS PAPER WORKS.
Mess.ʳˢ Charles Davidson & Sons, Lᵈ

Apart from fine writing papers and cardboard Aberdeen achieved some renown for the quality of its toilet paper, the 'Aristocrat of toilet tissue'. Hopefully 'Jean' found a roll in time.

began paper making, with Mugiemoss becoming the biggest manufacturer of paper bags in the world with branches across the UK and Australia and making the Davidsons immensely wealthy in the process. Another family closely associated with Aberdeen's paper industry was Pirie. In 1992 Pirie's merged with Wiggins Teape and Company.

After around 200 years of operating Culter mill closed *c.* 1980, the Donside mill closed in 2001, and Davidson's Mugiemoss mill shut in 2005. James Moir's Stoneywood mill has struggled to survive, but at the time of writing is still producing paper under a management buyout.

COMB MAKING

Aberdeen was Britain's centre of comb production, using thousands of tons of imported bone and shell. Nothing was wasted: cast-off chippings and parings were sold on to other industries, including confectioners who created pineapple flavouring from bone scrapings.

Numerous small comb works operated in the Rosemount area close to the largest of them all – Stewart's Aberdeen Comb Works on Hutcheon Street. Stewart's, which employed as many as 900 hands, began in a small way as Stuart & Rowell at King Street in the 1820s. At their peak Stewart's annual output of 9 million combs would extend over 700 miles if laid end to end.

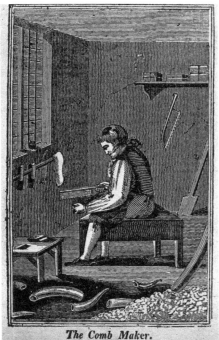

The Comb Maker.

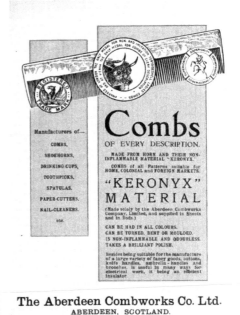

Above left: A pre-factory-age production print of a craft comb maker. (Courtesy of the Wellcome Collection under Creative Commons 4.0)

Above right: One step away from horn combs of the previous century, casein-based Keronyx was mass produced by the combworks in the 1920s.

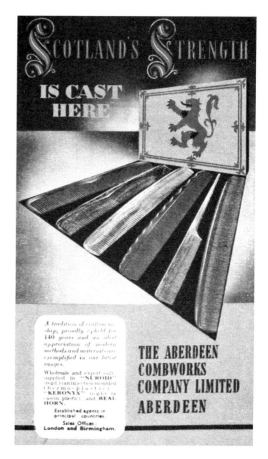

The combworks used its Scottish identity to promote products in the 1940s.

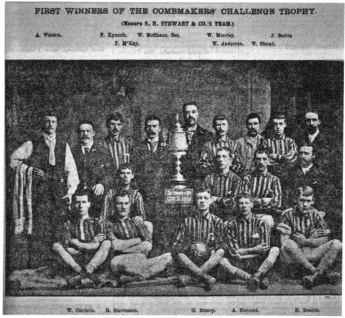

Combworks Football Challenge trophy, January 1893, contested between combworkers from Berryden and Hutcheon Street.

Combs were originally fashioned by hand – a difficult task simplified and sped up once machinery was introduced. By the 1820s mechanisation could turn out two combs from a single piece of horn or shell greatly cutting costs.

Comb workers were subject to a number of hazards. The razor-sharp tools tended to slip over hard bone and shell and the airborne powder residue from scraping bone was breathed into workers' lungs. It has been claimed, however, that during one cholera outbreak not a single comb maker in Aberdeen was affected – at least not fatally. Comb workers' deaths from congested lungs and associated illness, however, are not recorded.

HATTER

With his large waxed moustache and pointed beard the dapper figure of Samuel Martin, 'Hatter to the People', was familiar to Aberdonians. A self-promoter, Sammy Martin liked to present himself at his shop's first-floor window above Union Street shop dressed in a red Garibaldi shirt, riding breeches, boots with spurs and wielding a large cavalry sword. He smiled down at passers-by and curled his moustache. Martin's shop advertisements were no less flamboyant.

Martin's family were Lancashire weavers, but his father and brothers were army men. Martin's own fondness for the military led to his donation of an annual prize at the town's Wapinshaw for target shooting with an army Snyder rifle breech-loader, with shots at 2s a time.

The little hatter lies buried in Nellfield Cemetery. His imposing granite headstone is inscribed: 'The last resting place of Samuel Martin, Hatter to the People.' Stone and inscription were bought and carved years before Martin's death, with a blank space left for the date, which fell, unbeknown to him, on 7 January 1888. He was seventy-two years old.

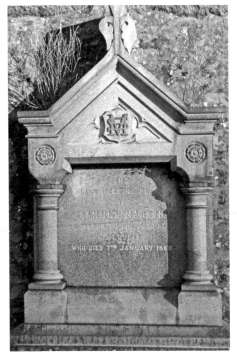

The Peoples' Hatter's grand memorial stone.

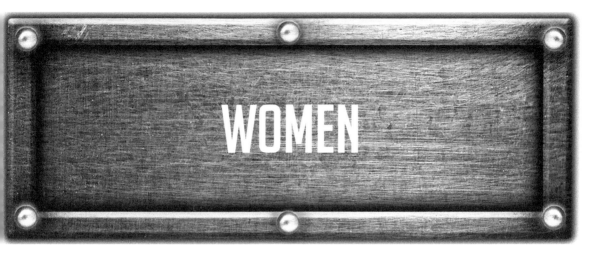

WOMEN

The second verse of William Carnie's 'A Factory Lassie's Song' referred to earlier mentions various female occupations:

> There's Peggy she's a polisher, Jean's at the envelopes,
> Flo and Kate wad fain be ladies, an' sae they serve in shops;
> Jemima stitches printed books, Miss Alice shoos at hame,
> Sly Annie cures provisions, and there's some I wadna name,
> There's some I wadna name, bit wi' a' their airt and skill,
> They canna ding the lassie oot that's wirkin' at the mill.

People sometimes have the impression that before the twentieth century women did not work. This is just wrong. Most women did work at some time outside the home; only well-off women did not. Women's work usually involved drudgery, long hours and very low pay – be they mill spinners, shop assistants or servants. As the verse suggests, where there were suitable alternatives women tended to prefer non-mill jobs, resulting in too few Aberdonian women willing to do mill and factory work. A degree of snobbishness surrounded mill employment, but women sometimes preferred the less than salubrious job of working in the fish to the mill, not from snobbery but because the work was flexible and paid by the hour. They were prepared to thole fish bree and cold for jobs that fitted in with family life.

Mill owners complained local women were overly fussy and too interested in frivolities such as going to the theatre and dancing, which kept them up late at night and meant they could not rise in time for early mill shifts.

Aberdeen was a prosperous city and some women were able to choose whether or not to work, bearing in mind their wages were often meagre. Those with an education might look to becoming clerkesses, governesses, teachers and, gradually, typists. Until the introduction of the typewriter at the turn of the nineteenth century men were chiefly employed in offices until women came to be increasingly hired for their deftness, intelligence and conscientiousness, or so it was claimed. Government and local government offices were first to employ 'lady typists' who initially came from middle-class families with civil service or military backgrounds. This changed with the growing popularity of typewriters in business offices. Nonetheless, females were still relegated to subordinate positions within office hierarchies and their popularity as

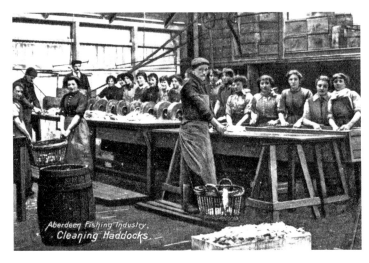

Edwardian postcard captures the gender division of 'working in the fish'.

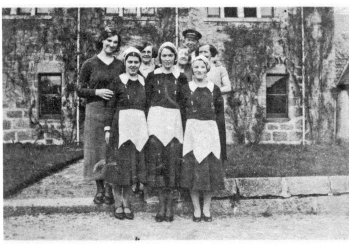

Domestic workers, employed by Aberdeen's Albyn School for Girls at their 'country retreat', Blelack House, 1930s.

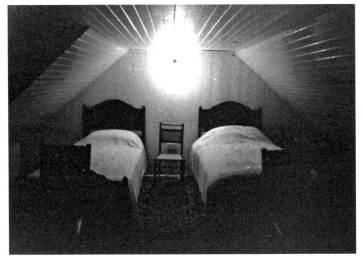

Attic farm bedroom, typical of the type of accommodation that live-in female servants occupied, without, of course, the electric light.

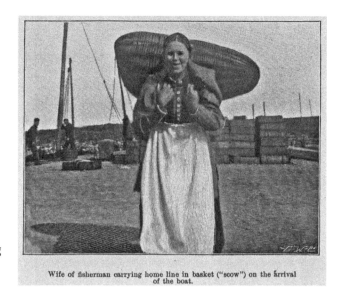

Wife of fisherman carrying home line in basket ("scow") on the arrival of the boat.

In Aberdeen and beyond selling fish was traditionally a job for women.

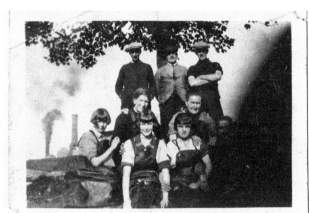

Fish quines (females) with male fellow workers between shifts, 1920s.

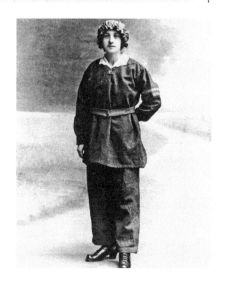

Margaret Craig from Torry in munitions workers' overalls, *c.* 1917. War work gave women unprecedented opportunities to move from the drudgery of domestic service into industry. Sadly Margaret died of influenza in 1919, aged twenty-one.

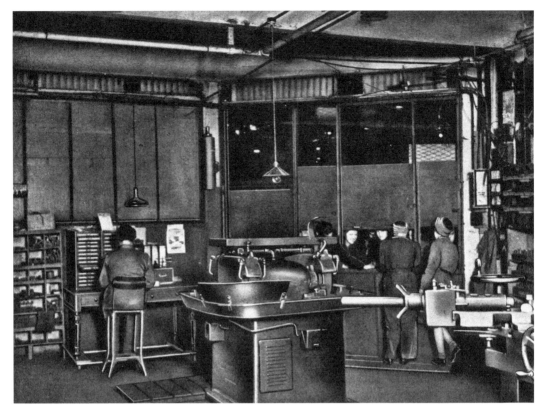

Women employed at J. M. Henderson's tool room in wartime, 1940s.

employees was not unconnected to that old story of women working for less pay than their male counterparts.

A curious type of female domestic employment that was common well before the days of mill work was one that met the needs of wealthy families while providing a respectable screen for the so-called 'sins' of 'errant' females. This was wet nursing. Aberdeen's high illegitimacy rate meant there were plenty available lactating women to act as wet nurses to infants of better-off women who were then freed from the 'toil' of breast feeding. Wet nurses were paid more than common servants – useful for any nurse fined by the Kirk for having 'sinned' by getting pregnant; and she, the nurse, was provided with bed and board at a time when otherwise she might find herself an outcast.

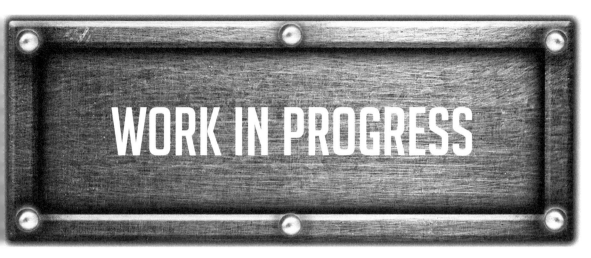

WORK IN PROGRESS

Aberdeen's commercial prosperity has more often than not centred on exploiting and harvesting local natural resources: wool spun and knitted by shank wives for export to Europe, salmon barrelled and sent abroad, grain grown or cattle selectively bred and sold at markets across Britain as beef, and bulls exported across the world to improve herd stocks. Aberdeen's central position at the centre of the country's white fishing industry came through the availability of local skills, its proximity to fishing grounds and its transport links (rail and maritime) across the length and breadth of the UK. Similar to the harvests from farming the fishing industry formed ties with other trades – engineering, ice making and ships' suppliers. But with the decline of local trawling in the 1970s fish sales declined and dependent local businesses and jobs such as fish market porters disappeared.

A similar fate was experienced by the great granite trade, which also harvested a local natural resource. Granite was a finite asset; once it was gone it was gone. Unlike white fish the stocks were not renewable. But so long as stone could be taken from the ground and worked at competitive prices while retaining quality the granite harvest sustained a buoyant industry. Indeed, as anyone walking across the north-east can testify, stone remains abundant and small harvests for decorative stone are still to be had in addition to greater volumes taken for roadstone. Market forces, however, mean bumper crops of dressed stone belong to the past.

Just as Aberdeen's fishing industry went into decline, the city was able to benefit from harvesting other natural resources – oil and gas. Their potential for creating wealth was far greater than generated from fishing vessels. Local shipbuilders formerly dependent on Aberdeen's fishing fleet adapted their skills and resources to meet the demands of multinational oil companies; for instance, converting trawlers to standby vessels for North Sea oil rigs, but oil and gas were different. The massive proportions of rigs and platforms precluded their construction in the city and Aberdeen's shipbuilders were unable to compete internationally for contracts to build specialist research and supply vessels.

The oil industry brought in new types of work and a strange exotic vocabulary: roustabouts, roughnecks, tool pushers and mud engineers. Wildcat no longer meant a Highland feline or spontaneous strike of workers, but an exploratory well in a potential oil or gas field. International companies arrived in Aberdeen to service and provide offshore activities, and local engineers and shipbuilders found themselves with opportunities to move to better-paid employment, albeit offshore and away from family and friends.

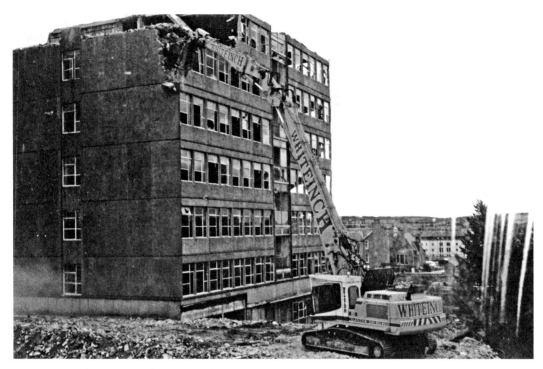

Demolition of Aberdeen College of Commerce on Holburn Street. Students and staff were evacuated at a moment's notice when the building was found to be in imminent danger of collapse, November 1987. (Courtesy of Jamie Dey)

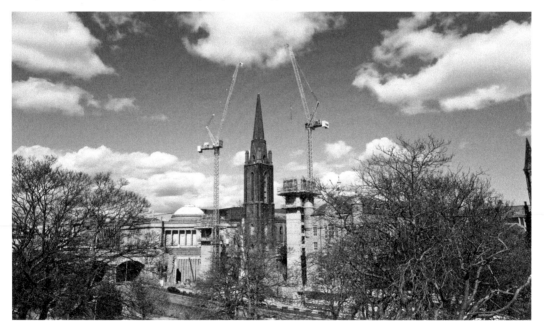

The red-brick steeple of the former Triple Kirks in granite Aberdeen gradually being enveloped by glass, steel and concrete of the twenty-first century.

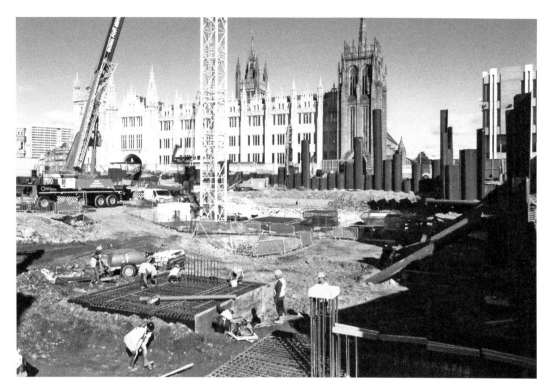

An all-too-brief moment in Aberdeen's architectural landscape when, following demolition of St Nicholas House, the magnificent granite façade of Marischal College was for the first and only time seen in all its glory.

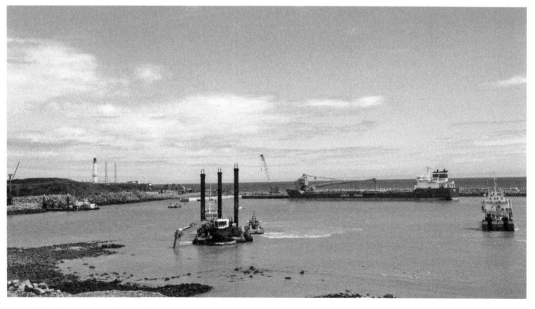

Harbour works at Nigg Bay. Dredging to create deep-water berthing facilities for large vessels, 2019.

Oil, like granite, is a finite resource and is harvested when potential profit outweighs production costs. The price of a barrel of oil is as volatile as the substance itself making job security uncertain. Aberdeen has experienced this insecurity, with local employment rising and falling dependent on the price of a barrel of Brent. Oil brought unprecedented work, prosperity and change to the city, but the status of oil is now under review for its impact on the climate. It has been exposed as Janus-faced along with that other fossil-fuel industry –coal. Both contributing to prosperity at the same time as environmental degradation.

Green energy is seen as the way forward, with global pressures to lower CO_2 emissions and on the face of it Aberdeen's oil status is threatened. To counter censure an Oil and Gas Technology Centre has been established to pursue better extractive technologies in oil and gas fields with diminishing resources. How successful this will be remains to be seen. Even with improved efficiency opposition to the exploitation of fossil fuels will remain.

The proliferation of elegant, if contentious, wind turbines across Aberdeenshire and elsewhere is a sign of the times. We are harvesting, in a sense, the power of wind to provide if not entirely a clean source of energy then one which, in part, can replace oil, gas and coal. The inevitable long-term decline of oil and gas sectors and the need to cut greenhouse gas emissions has led Aberdeen businesses to switch to servicing fledgling green technologies. In Aberdeen Bay there are now eleven graceful wind turbine generators. This project, funded by the European Union with the assistance of Aberdeen Renewable Energy Group, was promoted by the European Offshore Wind Group with Swedish company Vattenfall – the main contractor. The generators that went live in 2018 produce the equivalent of 70 per cent of Aberdeen's domestic electricity. How much local work will be generated by this new industry remains to be seen and whether there can be any large-scale transfer of skills and services from other sectors to this one is uncertain. Certainly, the Aberdeen Bay project has provided jobs for the city, not in manufacturing the huge windmills but, like Rigmar, in servicing and maintenance of wind turbines and power cables.

Aberdeen has a stake in the global phenomenon of harvesting green energy, but it is unclear if associated industries will provide levels of employment comparable to those provided by the town's former enterprises. Present times might be troubled, but the hairst of wind and wave power may yet help keep Aberdeen at work.

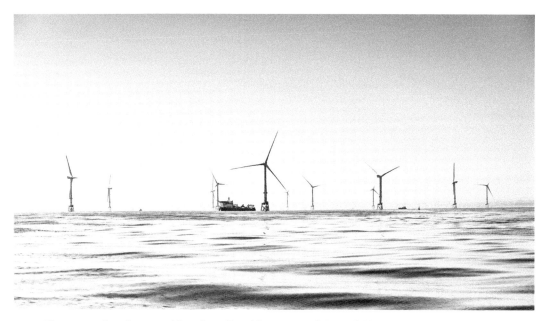

Eleven wind turbines in Aberdeen Bay. (Courtesy of Vattenfall)

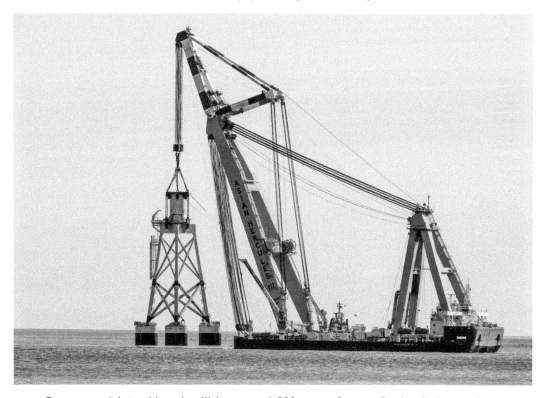

Crane vessel Asian Hercules III lowers a 1,800-tonne Suction Bucket Jacket to the seabed in Aberdeen Bay, one of eleven foundations installed to support wind turbine generators. (Courtesy of Vattenfall)

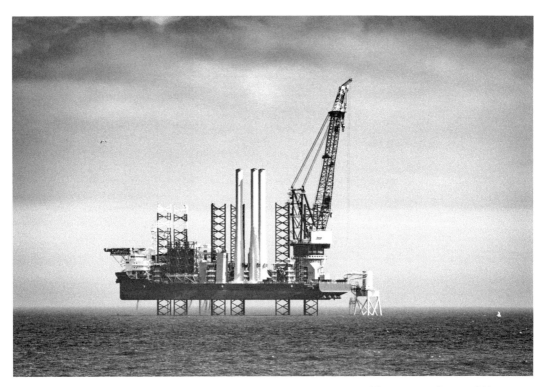

Erection of the upper structure of a wind turbine in Aberdeen Bay. (Courtesy of Vattenfall)

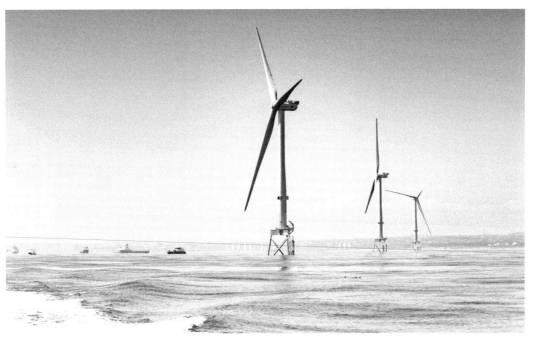

Looking towards Aberdeen and Seaton's high-rise blocks from wind turbine generators in Aberdeen Bay. (Courtesy of Vattenfall)